READ & SPEAK

GREEK

FOR BEGINNERS

SECOND EDITION

The Easiest Way to Learn to Communicate Right Away!

Series Concept
Jane Wightwick

Greek Edition
Hara Garoufalia-Middle • Howard Middle

Mc
Graw
Hill

New York Chicago San Francisco Lisbon London Madrid Mexico City
Milan New Delhi San Juan Seoul Singapore Sydney Toronto

Copyright © 2011 by g-and-w Publishing. All rights reserved. Printed in the United States of America. Except as permitted under the United States Copyright Act of 1976, no part of this publication may be reproduced or distributed in any form or by any means, or stored in a database or retrieval system, without the prior written permission of the publisher.

9 10 11 12 13 LHR 23 22 21 20

ISBN 978-0-07-176643-2 (book and CD package)
MHID 0-07-176643-X (book and CD package)

ISBN 978-0-07-176644-9 (book)
MHID 0-07-176644-8 (book)

Library of Congress Control Number 2010943203

Other titles in this series

Read & Speak Arabic for Beginners, 2nd Ed.
Read & Speak Chinese for Beginners, 2nd Ed.
Read & Speak Japanese for Beginners, 2nd Ed.
Read & Speak Korean for Beginners, 2nd Ed.

Related title

Your First 100 Words in Greek

McGraw-Hill books are available at special quantity discounts to use as premiums and sales promotion, or for use in corporate training programs. To contact a representative, please e-mail us at bulksales@mcgraw-hill.com.

This book is printed on acid-free paper.

Enhanced CD

The accompanying disk contains audio recordings that can be played on a standard CD player. These recordings are also included in MP3 format. For iPod or similar player:

1. Insert the disk into your computer
2. Open the disk via My Computer.
3. Drag the folder "MP3 files_Read & Speak Greek" into the Music Library of iTunes.
4. Sync your iPod with iTunes, then locate the files on your player under: ARTIST > Read & Speak Greek for Beginners, 2nd Ed.

Audio Flashcards

The Key Words vocabularies in this book can be studied online in interactive flashcard format at byki.com./listcentral. Search for "Read and Speak Greek" to locate the lists.

CONTENTS

PLUS...

- *8 tear-out cards for fun games*

- *Audio CD for listening and speaking practice*

- *Online activities to enhance learning*

Read & Speak GREEK

Welcome to *Read & Speak Greek*. This program will introduce you to the Greek language in easy-to-follow steps. The focus is on enjoyment and understanding, on *reading* words rather than writing them yourself. Through activities and games you'll learn how to read and speak basic Greek in less time than you thought possible.

You'll find these features in your program:

 Key Words See them written and hear them on the CD to improve your pronunciation.

 Language Focus Clear, simple explanations of language points to help you build up phrases for yourself.

? **Activities** Practice what you have learned through reading, listening, and speaking activities.

Games With tear-out components. Challenge yourself or play with a friend. A great, fun way to review.

Audio CD Hear the key words and phrases and take part in interactive listening and speaking activities. You'll find the track numbers next to the activities in your book.

If you want to give yourself extra confidence with reading the script, you will find *Your First 100 Words in Greek* the ideal pre-course companion to this program. *Your First 100 Words in Greek* introduces the Greek characters through 100 key everyday words, many of which also feature in *Read & Speak Greek*.

So now you can take your first steps in Greek with confidence, enjoyment and a real sense of progess.

Whenever you see the audio CD symbol, you'll find listening and speaking activities on your CD. The symbol shows the track number.

Track 1 is an introduction to the sounds of Greek, including an important feature on Greek tones. Listen to this before you start and come back to it again at later stages if you need to.

WHAT'S YOUR NAME?

 ## Key Words

2

Look at the script for each key word and try to visualize it, connecting its image to the pronunciation you hear on your CD.

γειά σας **yiá sas**	*hello* (polite)	Greek names:
γειά σου **yiá soo**	*hello* (informal)	Μαρία **maría** (female)
αντίο **adío**	*goodbye*	Άννα **ánna** (female)
		Κώστας **kóstas** (male)
το όνομά μου είναι...		
to ónomá moo íne...	*my name is…*	Γιώργος **yiórgos** (male)

The Greek alphabet has 24 characters. Many look and are pronounced similar to the English (Roman) alphabet; some look familiar but are pronounced differently; and some look and sound completely different. In general, Greek words can be pronounced exactly as they are written – unlike some English sounds such as "ough" as in rough, cough, through, though, etc. which all look the same but are pronounced differently.

Refer to the alphabet table on page 90 if you want to work out the individual letters in a word, but try to recognize the general shape of the words in Greek as you go along.

How do you say it?

Join the script to the pronunciation, as in the example.

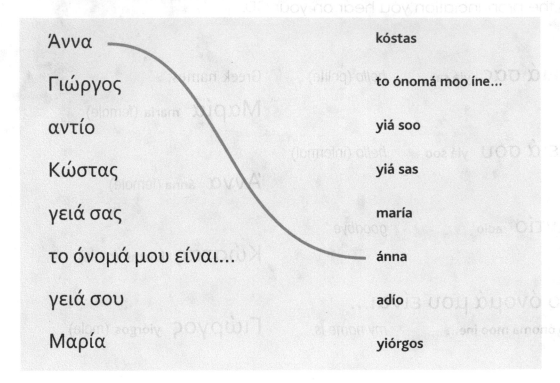

Άννα	kóstas
Γιώργος	to όnomá moo íne...
αντίο	yiá soo
Κώστας	yiá sas
γειά σας	maría
το όνομά μου είναι...	ánna
γειά σου	adío
Μαρία	yiórgos

What does it mean?

Now say the Greek out loud and write the English next to each.

γειά σας _hello (polite)_

Κώστας _____

Άννα _____

γειά σου _____

το όνομά μου είναι...
_____

αντίο _____

Γιώργος _____

Μαρία _____

Language Focus

In Greek, the word for "my" (or "your," "his," etc) comes after **όνομά ónomá** ("name"). "My name" is literally "the name my":

το όνομά μου είναι Άννα. to ónomá moo íne ánna
My name is Anna.

το όνομά μου είναι Κώστας. to ónomá moo íne kóstas
My name is Kostas.

As with some other languages, such as French, there are two ways in Greek of saying "you" or "your" – a polite way for people we don't know, and an informal way for friends, relatives and children. The polite way is also used when addressing more than one person (even if they are friends).

In Greek, **γειά σας yiá sas** means "your health," or literally "health your." The word **σας sas** is the polite way of saying "your" and is also used for more than one person. If you are only talking to one person you know well, use the informal word for "your," **σου soo**: **γειά σου yiá soo**.

Γειά σας, κύριε Γιώργο. yia sas, kírie yiórgo
Hello, Mr. Yiorgo.

Γειά σου, Μαρία. yia soo, maría
Hello, Maria.

Greek uses accent marks above vowels to show the stress, i.e. where you place the emphasis on a particular word. These marks will help you pronounce the words correctly.

 Practice introducing yourself and learn some useful replies on your CD.

3

What are they saying?

Write the correct number in the word balloons.

1 Γειά σας. Το όνομά μου
είναι Μαρία.
yiá soo. to ónomá moo íne maría

2 Γειά σου, Γιώργο.
yiá soo, yiorgo

3 Αντίο. **adío**

4 Γειά σου, Άννα.
yiá soo, anna

What do you hear?

Work out the phrases below. Then listen and check (✔)
the two phrases you hear on your audio CD.

4

1 Αντίο, Άννα. ☐

4 Γειά σας, Μαρία. ☐

2 Το όνομά μου είναι Κώστας. ☐

5 Γειά σας. ☐

3 Αντίο, Γιώργο. ☐

Key Words

5

Πώς είναι;
pos íne...? *what is...?*

Πώς είναι το όνομά σας;
pos íne to ónomá sas?
what is your name? (polite/plural)

Πώς είναι το όνομά σου;
pos íne to ónomá soo?
what is your name? (informal)

παρακαλώ
parakaló *please*

ευχαριστώ
efharistó *thank you*

καλημέρα
kaliméra *good morning*

καλησπέρα
kálispéra *good evening*

Language Focus

In the Greek script, a question mark looks like a semi-colon: **πώς;** *what?*

To form the question "What's your name?," the Greek follows the same pattern as English: **πώς** pos *what* + **είναι** íne *is* + **το όνομά σας** to ónoma sas *your name* (literally, "the name your").

If you are asking a child, you use the singular, informal word for "your," **σου** soo:

Γειά σου. Πώς είναι το όνομά σου;
yia soo. pos íne to ónomá soo?
Hello. What's your name?

Speaking practice

Practice the Greek you have learned so far.

6

What does it mean?

Match the English word balloons to the Greek.

For example: **1d**

1 Good morning.

2 Hello.

a Το όνομά μου είναι Μαρία.

b Παρακαλώ

3 What's your name?

4 Please.

c Ευχαριστώ.

d Καλημέρα.

5 My name's Maria.

6 Thank you.

e Πώς είναι το όνομά σας;

f Γειά σας.

Which word?

Write the correct number of the word in the box to complete the conversation, as in the example.

1 μου	4 όνομά
2 σπέρα	5 καλη
3 σας	6 είναι

Καλη __2__ .

Γειά σας, _____ σπέρα.

Το _____ μου _____ Άννα.

Πως είναι το όνομά _____ ;

Το όνονμά _____ είναι Γιώργος.

Language Focus

To say "Mr." and "Mrs." in Greek, we use **κύριος kírios** *(Mr.)* and **κυρία kiría** *(Mrs.)*. Notice that the stress changes. These words can be used with the first name or surname. There is no Greek equivalent of "Ms."

When you speak to a man and use the word for *Mr.*, it changes from **κύριος kírios** to **κύριε kírie**. In addition, the final **ς -s** is deleted from the name.

> Καλημέρα, κύριε Γιώργο.
> **kaliméra, kírie yiórgo**
> *Good morning, Mr. Yiorgo.*

What are their names?

Can you work out these common English names in Greek script?
Use the alphabet table on page 90 to help you work them out.

Κάθριν	*Catherine*	Τζων	_____
Μαίρη	_____	Ντέϊβιντ	_____
Ανν	_____	Μάικλ	_____
Ελίζαμπεθ	_____	Χάρρυ	_____

In or out?

Who is in the office today and who is out at meetings? Look at the wallchart and write the names in English in the correct column, as in the example.

Ελίζαμπεθ	✔
Τζων	✔
Άννα	✘
Χάρρυ	✔
Κώστας	✘
Μάϊκλ	✘
Κάθριν	✔
Ντέϊβιντ	✔
Γιώργος	✘
Μαίρη	✘

IN	OUT
Elizabeth	

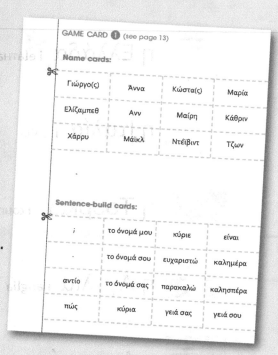

GAME CARD ① (see page 13)

Name cards:

Γιώργο(ς)	Άννα	Κώστα(ς)	Μαρία
Ελίζαμπεθ	Ανν	Μαίρη	Κάθριν
Χάρρυ	Μάϊκλ	Ντέϊβιντ	Τζων

Sentence-build cards:

;	το όνομά μου	κύριε	είναι
.	το όνομά σου	ευχαριστώ	καλημέρα
αντίο	το όνομά σας	παρακαλώ	καλησπέρα
πώς	κύρια	γειά σας	γειά σου

The Name Game

1. Tear out Game Card 1 at the back of your book and cut out the name cards (leave the sentence-build cards at the bottom of the sheet for the moment).

2. Put the cards Greek side up and see if you can recognize the names. Turn over the cards to see if you were correct.

3. Keep shuffling the cards and testing yourself until you can read all the names.

4. Then cut out the extra sentence-build cards at the bottom of the sheet and make mini-dialogs. For example:

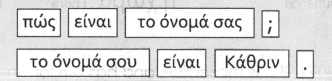

| πώς | είναι | το όνομά σας | ; |

| το όνομά σου | είναι | Κάθριν | . |

– pos íne to ónomá sas?

– to ónomá moo íne káthrin

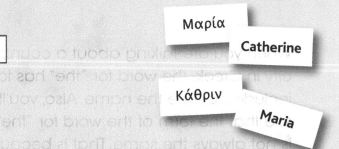

Μαρία

Catherine

Κάθριν

Maria

5. You can also play with a friend. Make mini-dialogs for each other to read. If you both have a book, you can play Pairs (pelmanism) with both sets of sentence-build cards, saying the words as you turn over the cards.

Key Words

η Ελλάδα **i elátHa**	*Greece*	
η Ιταλία **i italía**	*Italy*	
η Τουρκία · **i tourkía**	*Turkey*	
η Αγγλία **i anglía**	*England*	
η Αμερική **i amerikí**	*America*	

ο Καναδάς **o kanaτHás**	*Canada*	
η Ιρλανδία **i irlanτHía**	*Ireland*	
η Αυστραλία **i avstralía**	*Australia*	
η πόλη **i póli**	*city*	
η χώρα **i hóra**	*country*	

When you are talking about a country or city in Greek, the word for "the" has to be included before the name. Also, you'll see that the form of the word for "the" is not always the same. That is because in Greek there are three genders for all objects, names, places, etc.: masculine, feminine and neuter (see page 27 for more details). Most countries are feminine, so the word for "the" is **η i**. However, Canada is masculine, and has **ο o** for "the." The neuter word for "the" is **το to**. There are very few countries that have the neuter gender, but several cities are neuter, for example: **το Λονδίνο to lonτHíno** *London*.

Notice that **τH** in the pronunciation guide indicates the sound is like the "th" in "<u>th</u>at." Otherwise **th** is pronounced as in "<u>th</u>in."

Where are the countries?

Write the number next to the country, as in the example.

ο Καναδάς __1__	η Ελλάδα ___	η Αγγλία ___	η Ιταλία ___
η Ιρλανδία ___	η Αμερική ___	η Τουρκία ___	η Αυστραλία ___

How do you say it?

Join the English to the pronunciation and the Greek script, as in the example.

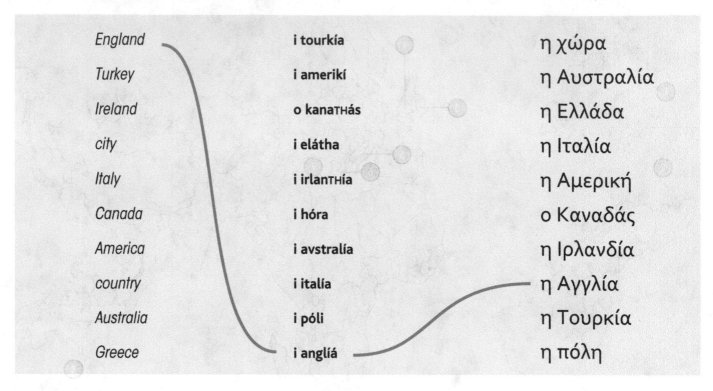

English	i tourkía	η χώρα
Turkey	i amerikí	η Αυστραλία
Ireland	o kanaτHás	η Ελλάδα
city	i elátha	η Ιταλία
Italy	i irlanτHía	η Αμερική
Canada	i hóra	ο Καναδάς
America	i avstralía	η Ιρλανδία
country	i italía	η Αγγλία
Australia	i póli	η Τουρκία
Greece	i anglía	η πόλη

Where are the cities?

Read the Language Focus on page 17 before you try this activity. Then look at these cities and make sentences about where they are as in the example.

Το Λονδίνο είναι στην Αγγλία.

to lonτHíno íne stin anglía *[The] London is in [the] England.*

Athens	New York	Washington	Ankara
η Αθήνα	η Νέα Υόρκη	η Ουάσινκγτον	η Αγκύρα
i athína	i nea yórki	i ouásington	i ángira

Thessaloniki	Sydney	London	Dublin
η Θεσσαλονίκη	το Σίντνεϊ	το Λονδίνο	το Δουβλίνο
i thessaloníki	to sídnei	to lonτHíno	to τHoovlíno

Language Focus

It is straightforward to say where you are from. Use the phrase Εγώ είμαι από... **egó íme apó...** *I am from...* and add the name of the country or town. The masculine and feminine words for "the" change from **o o** and **η i** to **τον ton** and **την tin** after **από apó**. The neuter **το to** stays the same.

> Εγώ είμαι από την Ελλάδα.
> **egó íme apó tin eláτна**   *I am from [the] Greece.*
>
> Εγώ είμαι από τον Καναδά.
> **egó íme apo ton kanaτнá**   *I am from [the] Canada.*

To say "in," we use **σε se**, which becomes simply **σ s** when you put it in front of **την tin, τον ton**, or **το to**: σε + την/τον/το = στην/στον/στο.

> Εγώ είμαι από την Ουάσινκγτον, στην Αμερική.
> **egó íme apo ton ouásington, stin amerikí**
> *I am from [the] Washington, in [the] America.*

To say "near," we use the word **κοντά kondá** in front of the phrase for "in the":

> Εγώ είμαι από την Οξφόρδη, μία πόλη κοντά
> στο Λονδίνο.
> **egó íme apo tin oksfórτнi, mia póli kondá sto lonτнíno**
> *I am from [the] Oxford, a city near [the] London.*

If you want to ask someone where they are from, you need to use the question:
Από πού είστε εσείς; **apo poo íste esís?** *From where are you?*

> Από πού είστε εσείς, Μαρία;
> **apo poo iste esís, maría?**   *Where are you from, Maria?*

Listen to four different people introducing themselves and see if you can understand where they are from.

8

Where are they from?

Join the people to their nationalities, as in the example. Listen again to track 8 on your CD and look back at the names and countries if you need to remind yourself.

Maria	η Ιταλία
Michael	ο Καναδάς
Susan	η Αμερική
Selim	η Αγγλία
Nicoletta	η Ελλάδα
Stuart	η Τουρκία

Where are you from?

Now say where you're from.
Follow the prompts on your audio CD.

9

 Key Words

10

εγώ είμαι	egó íme	I am	αυτός είναι	aftós íne	he is
εσείς είστε esís íste		you are (polite/plural)	αυτή είναι	aftí íne	she is
			από	apó	from
εσύ είσαι esí íse		you are (informal)	πού;	poo?	where?

 *Language Focus*

You now know how to ask and answer questions about where you're from:

Από πού είστε; **apo poo íste?**
Where are you from?

Είμαι από την Ελλάδα. **íme apo tin elátHa**
I am from Greece.

Notice that the question and answer above doesn't include the words for "I"
(εγώ **egó**) or "you" (εσείς/εσύ **esís/esí**). In Greek we don't usually need to
include these words as the form of the verb already tells us who is speaking.

If you want to talk about where someone else is from, you use αυτός **aftós** *(he)*
or αυτή **aftí** *(she)*:

Από πού είναι αυτός; **apó poo íne aftós?**
Where's he from?

Αυτός είναι από την Αμερική.
aftós íne apó tin amerikí
He's from America.

Από πού είναι αυτή; **apó poo íne aftí?**
Where's she from?

Αυτή είναι από την Αθήνα, στην Ελλάδα.
aftí íne apó tin athína, stin elátHa
She's from Athens, in Greece.

Remember that in Greek the word for "the" has to go in front of the city or country
with the masculine and feminine words changing from **o** o and **η** i, to **τον** ton
and **την** tin after a preposition like από **apó**. The neuter **το** to stays the same.

Who's from where?

Make questions and answers about where these people are from, as in the example.

1

Από πού είναι αυτός;
apó poo íne aftós?
Where's he from?

Αυτός είναι από την Νέα
Υόρκη, στην Αμερική.
**aftós íne apó tin Néa Yórki,
stin Amerikí**
He is from New York, in America.

2

3

4

5

6

7

8

Listen and check

Listen to the conversation on your audio CD and decide if these sentences are true or false.

		True	False
1	The woman's name is Sophie.	☐	☐
2	She comes from Canada.	☐	☐
3	The man's name is Yiorgos.	☐	☐
4	He comes from Greece.	☐	☐
5	They are already friends.	☐	☐

What does it mean?

Now read the Greek you heard in the conversation and match it with English, as in the example.

I'm from Canada.	Το όνομά μου είναι Λούσυ.
He's from Greece.	Εγώ είμαι από τον Καναδά.
My name's Lucy.	Γειά σας.
What's your name?	Πώς είναι το όνομά σας;
Good evening.	Αυτός είναι από την Ελλάδα.
Hello.	Καλησπέρα

What does it mean?

Try to work out each of these sentences. It will help if you break them up into the separate words and phrases. Look back at the Key Word panels if you need help.

Then read the sentences out loud when you have figured them out and write the English next to each, as in the example.

1 Το όνομά μου είναι Λούσυ.   *My name is Lucy.*

2 Είμαι από τον Καναδά.   _____

3 Ο Κώστας είναι από την Ελλάδα.   _____

4 Πώς είναι το όνομά σας;   _____

5 Το όνομά μου είναι Μαρία.   _____

6 Από πού είναι αυτός;   _____

7 Αυτός είναι από την Αγγλία.   _____

8 Αυτή είναι από την Αμερική.   _____

You can compare your pronunciation of the sentences with the models on your audio CD.

12

Now complete this description of yourself, adding your own details.
Then say the description out loud.

Το όνομά μου είναι... (name).

Εγώ είμαι από τον/την/το... (city/town) στον/στιν/στο... (country).

The Flag Game

1. Tear out Game Card 2.

2. Find a die and counter(s).

3. Put the counter(s) on START.

4. Throw the die and move that number of squares.

5. When you land on a flag, you must ask and answer the appropriate question for that country. For example:

Από πού είστε; **apó poo íste?**
Where are you from?

Εγώ είμαι από την Αγγλία.
íme apó tin anglía
I am from England.

6. If you can't remember the question or answer, you must go back to the square you came from. You must throw the exact number to finish.

7. You can challenge yourself or play with a friend.

Key Words

η καρέκλα **i karékla**	*chair*	η πόρτα **i pórta**	*door*
το τραπέζι **to trapézi**	*table*	το παράθυρο **to paráthiro**	*window*
η τηλεόραση **i tileórasi**	*television*	το στιλό **to stiló**	*pen*
το βιβλίο **to vivlío**	*book*	το περιοδικό **to perioΤΗΙκó**	*magazine*
η τσάντα **i tsánta**	*bag*	ο καναπές **o kanapés**	*sofa*
το κομπιούτερ **to kompiúter**	*computer*	το τηλέφωνο **to tiléfono**	*telephone*

13

Listen first to the key words on your CD. Then look around the room you're in and try to use the words to name as many objects as you can find. Count how many Greek words you use.

Then look back at the list and review the words you couldn't remember. Try again to name objects and see if you can beat your first score.

What does it mean?

Match the Greek with the pictures, then write the pronunciation and the English, as in the example.

το περιοδικό

το βιβλίο

η πόρτα

το παράθυρο   *to paráthiro window*

το στιλό

η καρέκλα

το τραπέζι

η τηλεόραση

το τηλέφωνο

η τσάντα

ο καναπές

το κομπιούτερ

Word Square

Can you find the seven key words in the word square? Circle them and write the English, as in the example. The words can be horizontal or vertical.

τ	ρ	α	π	έ	ζ	ι	β
η	ί	τ	ό	κ	έ	λ	ι
λ	ο	σ	ρ	α	η	ν	β
έ	ρ	ά	τ	ν	τ	ι	λ
φ	έ	ν	α	α	ο	β	ί
ω	κ	τ	ρ	π	κ	λ	ο
ν	κ	α	ρ	έ	κ	λ	α
ο	ω	ν	έ	ς	σ	ο	η

sofa

_____

_____

_____

_____

_____

_____

Odd One Out

Which is the odd one out? Circle the word that doesn't belong in each row.

κομπιούτερ * παράθυρο * καλημέρα * τηλεόραση

η πόρτα * η Ελλάδα * η Αμερική * η Αγγλία

βιβλίο * όνομα * περιοδικό * στιλό

πόλη * καναπές * καρέκλα * τραπέζι

καλησπέρα * γειά σας * καλημέρα * καρέκλα

Language Focus

We have seen that Greek words have three genders: masculine, feminine and neuter. You can't automatically tell what gender a word is, although you will start to spot similarities.

The words for "the" and "a" in Greek change according to the gender of the words they refer to (and whether they are singular or plural). The three singular words for "the" are **o** o (masculine), **η** i (feminine), and **το** to (neuter). The singular words for "a" are **ένας énas** (masculine), **μία mía** (feminine), and **ένα éna** (neuter):

masculine	feminine	neuter
o/ένας καναπές **o/énas kanapés** *(sofa)*	**η/μία πόρτα** **i/mía pórta** *(door)*	**το/ένα βιβλίο** **to/éna vivlío** *(book)*
o/ένας φούρνος **o/énas foúrnos** *(stove)*	**η/μία τηλεόραση** **i/mía tileórasi** *(TV)*	**το/ένα όνομα** **to/éna ónoma** *(name)*
o/ένας καφές **o/énas kafés** *(coffee)*	**η/μία τσάντα** **i/mía tsánta** *(bag)*	**το/ένα στιλό** **to/éna stiló** *(pen)*

To ask what something is, use the phrase: **Τι είναι αυτό; ti íne aftó?** *What is it?* The reply would begin **Είναι... íne...** *(It's...)* followed by what it is with the appropriate form of "a." Note that you don't need to repeat the word for "it" in your answer.

Τι είναι αυτό; ti íne aftó? *What is it?*

Είναι ένα στιλό. íne éna stiló *It's a pen.*

You can also ask a yes/no question using **Αυτό είναι...; aftó íne...** *(Is it...?).* The word for "yes" is **ναι ne**, and "no" is **όχι óhi.**

Αυτό είναι ένα περιοδικό; aftó íne éna perioтнikó? *Is it a magazine?*

Ναι. Είναι ένα περιοδικό./Όχι. Είναι ένα βιβλίο.
ne. íne éna perioтнikó/ohi. íne éna vivlío *Yes. It's a magazine./No, it's a book.*

Your turn to speak

Now ask what things are. Follow the prompts on your audio CD.

14

What is it?

Look at the photos of everyday objects from unusual angles. Then read the sentences and decide which picture they describe, as in the example.

1 Είναι μία καρέκλα. _e_

5 Είναι μία πόρτα. __

2 Είναι ένα κομπιούτερ. __

6 Είναι μία τηλεόραση. __

3 Είναι ένας καναπές. __

7 Είναι ένα στιλό. __

4 Είναι ένα τηλέφωνο. __

8 Είναι μία τσάντα. __

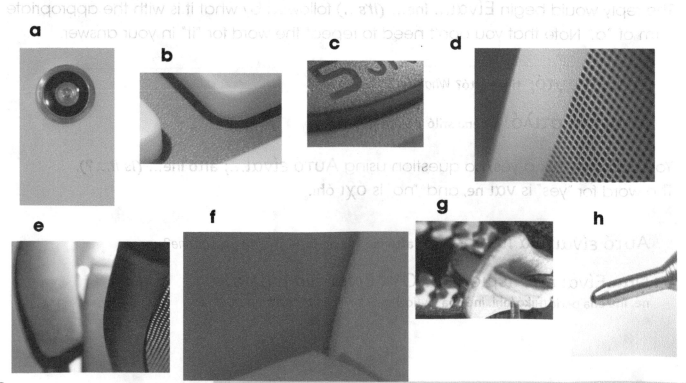

a

b

c

d

e

f

g

h

 ## Key Words

το τσάϊ	to tsai	tea	το παγωτό	to pagotó	ice cream
ο καφές	o kafés	coffee	το σάντουϊτς		sandwich
			to sándouits		
το κέϊκ	to keik	cake			
			η τυρόπιττα		cheese pie
το γλυκό	to glikó	sweet	i tirópitta		

Language Focus

The easiest way to ask for something in a café or shop is to use the word **θέλω**
thélo *(I want/I would like).* If you want something else, just add **και ke** *(and).*
It is not impolite in Greek simply to say "I want," rather than "May/Can I have?"

Θέλω ένα τσάϊ, παρακαλώ. thélo éna tsai, parakaló
I want/I'd like a tea, please.

Θέλω ένα κέϊκ και μια τυρόπιττα, παρακαλώ.
thélo éna keik ke mia tirópitta, parakaló
I want/I'd like a cake and a cheese pie, please.

Masculine words such as **καφές kafés** lose the final **-s** after **θέλω thélo.**
The word for "a" also changes from **ένας énas** to **έναν énan**:

Θέλω έναν καφέ. thélo énan kafé *I want/I'd like a coffee.*

Having asked for an item you may hear the word **ορίστε oríste** *(here you are)*:

Θέλω ένα σάντουϊτς, παρακαλώ.
thélo éna sandouits, parakaló *I want a sandwich, please.*

Ορίστε, κυρία. oríste, kiría *Here you are, Madam.*

Who orders what?

What are the customers ordering? Listen to your CD
and check what they order, as in the example.

16

	tea	coffee	sandwich	cake	cheese pie	ice cream	sweet
Customer 1		✓	✓				
Customer 2							
Customer 3							
Customer 4							
Customer 5							

Now look at the table above and pretend you are ordering for yourself.

Θέλω έναν καφέ και ένα σάντουϊτς, παρακαλώ.

thélo énan kafé ke éna sándouits, parakaló

Unscramble the conversation

Can you put this conversation in the correct order?

a Γειά σας. Θέλω έναν καφέ.
yia sas. thélo énan kafé.

b Ευχαριστώ.
efharistó

c Ναι. Και τι είναι αυτό;
ne. ke ti íne aftó?

d Ορίστε. Έναν καφέ, και μια τυρόπιττα.
oríste. énan kafé ke mía tirópitta

e Έναν καφέ;
enan kafé?

f Είναι μία τυρόπιττα.
íne mía tirópitta

g Καλημέρα.
kaliméra

h Μία τυρόπιττα, παρακαλώ.
mía tirópitta, parakaló

ORDER: _g._ _____

Now check your answer with the
conversation on your audio CD.

17

At the café

Your turn to order now. Look at the menu below and then you'll be
ready to order from the waiter on your CD.

τσάι

καφές

σάντουϊτς

κέϊκ

γλυκό

τυρόπιττα

παγωτό

The Café Game

1. Cut out the picture cards from Game Card 3.

2. Put the cards into a bag.

3. Shake the bag.

4. Pull out a card without looking.

5. Ask for the item on the card. For example:

   Θέλω ένα τσάϊ, παρακαλώ.

   thélo éna tsai, parakaló
   I want a tea, please.

6. If you can ask the question out loud quickly and fluently, then put the card aside. If not, then put it back into the bag.

7. See how long it takes you to get all of the cards out of the bag. Or play with a friend and see who can collect the most cards.

GAME CARD 3 (see page 33)

Picture cards:

Key Words

το δωμάτιο **to THomátio**	*room*	το ντουλάπι **to doulápi**		*cupboard*
το ψυγείο **to psiyío**	*refrigerator*	το δέντρο **to THéndro**		*tree*
η κουρτίνα **i kourtína**	*curtain*	το αυτοκίνητο **to aftokínito**		*car*
ο φούρνος **o foúrnos**	*stove*			
το κρεβάτι **to kreváti**	*bed*	η γάτα **i gáta**		*cat*
το κάδρο **to káTHro**	*picture*	ο σκύλος **o skílos**		*dog*
το σπίτι **to spíti**	*house*	το ποντίκι **to pondíki**		*mouse*

19

You'll see in the list above that most of the words are neuter, but four are not. Can you pick out the masculine and feminine words? What helped you do this?

You can make some helpful hints for yourself for identifying gender.

For example, *most* words that end in **-o** are neuter, *most* that end in **-ος** are masculine and *most* that end in **-α** are feminine. However, don't turn these hints into hard-and-fast rules. There are plenty of exceptions.

What does it mean?

Join the Greek to the pronunciation and write down the meaning in English.

Greek	Pronunciation	Meaning
ο φούρνος	to kreváti	
το κρεβάτι	to káτHro	
το κάδρο	to spíti	
ο σκύλος	to τHomátio	
το ποντίκι	o foúrnos	*stove*
το σπίτι	to psiyío	
το ντουλάπι	i gáta	
το δέντρο	to pondíki	
το αυτοκίνητο	to doulápi	
το δωμάτιο	i kourtína	
το ψυγείο	to τHéndro	
η κουρτίνα	to aftokínito	
η γάτα	o skílos	

What can you see?

Look at the picture and check (✔) the things you can see, as in the example.

γάτα ✔ ψυγείο ☐
σκύλος ☐ παράθυρο ☐
φούρνος ☐ κρεβάτι ☐
τραπέζι ☐ κουρτίνα ☐
στιλό ☐ ποντίκι ☐
βιβλίο ☐ πόρτα ☐
περιοδικό ☐ κάδρο ☐
κομπιούτερ ☐ ντουλάπι ☐
τσάντα ☐ καρέκλα ☐

 Key Words

σε se	*in/on*	**μπροστά από** brostá apó	*in front of*
μέσα σε mesa se	*inside*		
κάτω από káto apó	*under*	**πίσω από** píso apó	*behind*
πάνω από páno apó	*above*	**δίπλα σε** ΤΗípla se	*next to*

Language Focus

In Greek, prepositions ("position" words) are followed by a different form of the word for "the" or "a." The "normal" (subject) forms of "the" and "a" are shown on page 27. After a preposition, the masculine **ο o** becomes **τον ton**, the feminine **η i** becomes **την tin**, but the neuter **το to** stays the same. Sometimes the ending of the following word will also change slightly, e.g. **ο καναπές o kanapés** *(the sofa)* but **κάτω από τον καναπέ káto apó ton kanapé** *(under the sofa)*.

When you use the preposition **σε se** *(in/on)* with the word for "the," it combines to produce **στον/στην/στο ston/stin/sto**.

Η γάτα είναι κάτω από τον καναπέ.
i gáta íne káto apó ton kanapé *The cat is under the sofa.*

Το στιλό είναι στο τραπέζι.
to stiló íne sto trapézi *The pen is on the table.*

Practice saying where things are on your CD.

21

Which word?

Put a circle around the word that correctly describes each picture, as in the example.

Το αυτοκίνητο είναι ⟨**μπροστά από**⟩ το σπίτι.
πίσω από

πάνω από
Το κρεβάτι είναι   το παράθυρο.
κάτω από

μπροστά από
Το κάδρο είναι   τον καναπέ.
πάνω από

σ(ε)
Το κομπιούτερ είναι   το τραπέζι.
δίπλα σ(ε)

πίσω από
Η γάτα είναι   την καρέκλα.
κάτω από

δίπλα σ(ε)
Το ψυγείο είναι   τον φούρνο.
πάνω από

μέσα σ(ε)
Ο σκύλος είναι   το αυτοκίνητο.
επάνω σ(ε)

Language Focus

A useful phrase in Greek to say what there is in a place is **υπάρχει** ipárhi *there is*:

> Υπάρχει ένα κομπιούτερ στο τραπέζι.
> **ipárhi éna kompiúter sto trapézi**
> *There's a computer on the table.*
>
> Υπάρχει μια τηλεώραση δίπλα στον καναπέ.
> **ipárhi mía tileórasi THípla ston kanapé**
> *There's a television next to the sofa.*
>
> Υπάρχει ένα κάδρο κάτω από το παράθυρο.
> **ipárhi éna káTHro káto apó to paráthiro**
> *There's a picture under the window.*

If you want to ask the question **Is there a ...?**, you can use the same phrase, raising your voice at the end.

> Υπάρχει μια τηλεώραση στο δωμάτιο;
> **ipárhi mía tileórasi sto THomátio?**
> *Is there a television in the room?*

> Look around the room you are in at the moment, or think of a room you know well. Can you describe where some of the things are, using **υπάρχει...** ipárhi...?

Where are the mice?

See how many mice you can find in the picture and make sentences about them using the sentence table, as in the example.

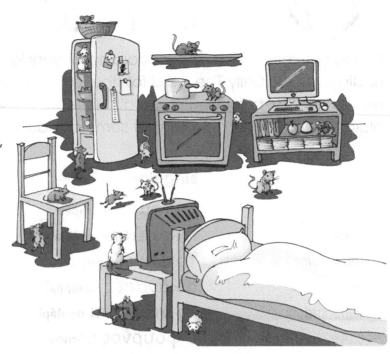

Example:

Υπάρχει ένα ποντίκι μπροστά από το ψυγείο.

ipárhi éna pondiki brostá apó to psiyío
There's a mouse in front of the refrigerator.

		το τραπέζι.
	μέσα σ(ε)	την καρέκλα.
	πάνω από	το ψυγείο.
	κάτω από	τον καναπέ.
Υπάρχει ένα ποντίκι	πίσω από	το ντουλάπι.
	σ(ε)	τον φούρνο.
	δίπλα σ(ε)	την τηλεόραση.
	μπροστά από	το κομπιούτερ.
		το κρεβάτι.

Language Focus

Plurals of Greek words vary according to gender, so you will need to learn their endings individually. The word for "the" also changes to **οι i** for masculine and feminine plurals and **τα ta** for neuter plurals. Here are some words you know already with their plurals. You may be able to spot some similarities in the plural patterns.

	singular	**plural**
table	το τραπέζι trapézi	τα τραπέζια trapézya
chair	η καρέκλα karékla	οι καρέκλες karékles
refrigerator	το ψυγείο psiyío	τα ψυγεία psiyía
sofa	ο καναπές kanapés	οι καναπέδες kanapéthes
cupboard	το ντουλάπι doolápi	τα ντουλάπια doolápya
stove	ο φούρνος foúrnos	οι φούρνοι foúrni
television	η τηλεόραση tileórasi	οι τηλεοράσεις tileórasis
bed	το κρεβάτι kreváti	τα κρεβάτια krevátya
book	το βιβλίο vivlío	τα βιβλία vivlía
bag	η τσάντα tsánda	οι τσάντες sándes
door	η πόρτα pórta	οι πόρτες pórtes
window	το παράθυρο paráthiro	τα παράθυρα paráthira
pen	το στιλό stiló	τα στιλό* stiló (*no change)
room	το δωμάτιο THomátio	τα δωμάτια THomátya
curtain	η κουρτίνα koortína	οι κουρτίνες koortínes
picture	το κάδρο káTHro	τα κάδρα káTHra
house	το σπίτι spíti	τα σπίτια spítya
tree	το δέντρο THéndro	τα δέντρα THéndra
dog	ο σκύλος skílo	οι σκύλοι skíli
cat	η γάτα gáta	οι γάτες gátes
mouse	το ποντίκι pondíki	τα ποντίκια pondíkya

Note that **υπάρχει ipárhi** *(there is)* changes to **υπάρχουν ipárhoon** *(there are)* if you are talking about more than one thing: Υπάρχουν βιβλία στο ντουλάπι. **ipárhoon vivlía sto doulápi** *(There are books in the cupboard.)*

You can make a sentence negative in Greek by inserting the word **δεν** ᴛʜᴇn (*not*) in front of the verb. For example:

Είμαι απο την Αγγλια. Δεν είμαι από την Αμερική.
íme apó tin anglía. ᴛʜᴇn íme apó tin amerikí
I am from England. I am not from America.

Δεν υπάρχει ένα κονπιούτερ στο δομάτιο.
ᴛʜᴇn ipárhi éna kompiúter sto ᴛʜomátio
There isn't a computer in the room.

Listen and learn

You'll find an activity on your CD to help you remember the plurals.

22

True or False?

Decide if the sentences describing the picture are true or false, as in the example.

		True	False
1	Υπάρχει ένα ψυγείο στο δωμάτιο.	☑	☐
2	Υπάρχει ένα κρεβάτι στο δωμάτιο.	☐	☐
3	Το τηλέφωνο είναι στο τραπέζι.	☐	☐
4	Δεν υπάρχουν ντουλάπια.	☐	☐
5	Υπάρχουν παράθυρα.	☐	☐
6	Δεν υπάρχει ένα ποντίκι κάτω από το τραπέζι.	☐	☐
7	Υπάρχουν δέντρα πίσω από το σπίτι.	☐	☐
8	Ο φούρνος είναι δίπλα στο ψυγείο.	☐	☐
9	Υπάρχει ένας σκύλος κάτω από το τραπέζι.	☐	☐
10	Δεν υπάρχει μια τηλεόραση στο δωμάτιο.	☐	☐

Language Review

You're half way through *Read & Speak Greek for Beginners* – congratulations!
This is a good time to summarize the main language points covered so far.

1 Greek has three genders: masculine, feminine and neuter. You can often tell the gender of a word by its ending. Some masculine nouns end in **-ος -os**; some feminine nouns in **-α -a** or **-η -i**; some neuter nouns in **-ο -o**.

2 The words for "a" and "the" (articles) change according to the gender. When the person or object is the subject of the sentence, the forms of the articles are:

article	masculine	feminine	neuter
a/an	ένας énas	μία mía	ένα éna
the	Ο o	η i	ΤΟ to

Υπάρχει ένας φουρνος δίπλα στο ψυγείο.
iparhi énas foúrnos тнípla sto psiyío
There's a stove next to the refrigerator.

Υπάρχει μία τσάντα και ένα στιλό στο ντουλάπι.
iparhi mia tsanda ke éna stiló sto doolápi
There's a bag and a pen in the cupboard.

3 When the noun is not the subject of the sentence, the articles can change:

article	masculine	feminine	neuter
a/an	έναν énan	μία mía	ένα éna
the	ΤΟΝ ton	την tin	ΤΟ to

Θέλω έναν καφέ, παρακαλώ.
thélo énan kafé, parakaló *I'd like a coffee. please.*

Είμαι από την Αθήνα.
íme apó tin athína *I'm from (the) Athens.*

4 Plurals vary but there are some patterns: masculine nouns ending in **-ος** form the plural with **-οι**; feminine nouns ending in **-α** or **-η** form the plural with **-ες -es**; neuter nouns ending in **-ο** form the plural with **-α -a** (see page 40).

My Room

(1) Tear out Game Card 4 at the back of your book and cut out the small pictures of items around the house (leave the sentence-build cards at the bottom of the sheet for the moment).

(2) Stick the pictures wherever you like on the scene below.

(3) Cut out the sentence-build cards from Game Card 4. Make as many sentences as you can describing your room. For example:

Υπάρχει	ένα κάδρο	πάνω από το	κρεβάτι	.

iparhi éna kátηro páno apó to kreváti

There's a picture above the bed.

Sentence-build cards:			
πάνω από τον	δίπλα στον	κάτω από τον	στ
πάνω από το	δίπλα στο	κάτω από το	στ
πάνω από την	δίπλα στην	κάτω από την	στ
καναπές	κρεβάτι	τραπέζι	καρέ
ένα σάντουϊτς	ένα κάδρο	ένα τηλέφωνο	ένα κομπι
Υπάρχει	μία γάτα	ένα ποντίκι	μία τηλεόρε

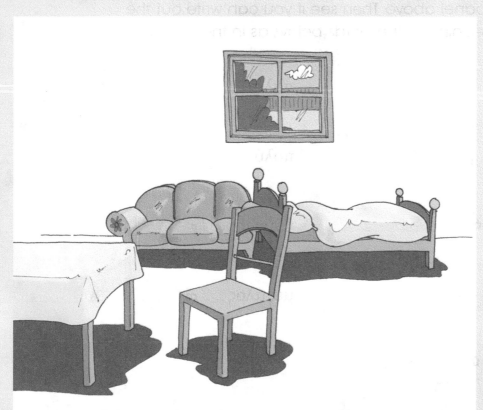

Key Words

μεγάλος	megálos	big	ακριβός	akrivós	expensive
μικρός	micrós	small	φτηνός	ftinós	inexpensive
παλιός	paliós	old	αργός	argós	slow
καινούριος	kenoórios	new	γρήγορος	grígoros	fast
πολύ	polí	very			

Can you remember?

Cover the Key Words panel above. Then see if you can write out the pronunciation and meaning of the words below, as in the example.

αργός	a r g ó s slow	παλιός	p _ _ _ _ _ _ _ _ _ _
μικρός	m _ _ _ _ _ s _ _ _ _ _ _	πολύ	_ _ _ í _ _ _ _ _ _
φτηνός	f _ _ _ ó _ _ _ _ _ _ _	γρήγορος	g _ í _ _ r _ _ _ _ _ _ _
ακριβός	_ k _ _ _ ó _ _ _ _ _ _ _	μεγάλος	m _ _ _ l _ _ _ _ _ _ _
καινούριος	_ e _ _ ú _ _ _ _ _ _		

Language Focus

In Greek, descriptive words (adjectives) come before the word they are describing, as they do in English:

> ένας μεγάλος σκύλος **énas megalos skílos** *a big dog*
>
> ο παλιός καναπές **o paliós kanapés** *the old sofa*

Adjectives change their ending depending on the gender of the word they describe. The adjectives shown in the panel on page 44 are masculine. In general, adjectives that end in **-ος (-os)** for masculine words will change to **-η (-i)** or **-α (-a)** when describing feminine words and to **-ο (-o)** for neuter words.

> η μεγάλη καρέκλα **i megáli karékla** *the big chair* (fem.)
>
> ένα μεγάλο σπίτι **éna megálo spíti** *a big house* (neut.)
>
> μία παλιά τσάντα **mía paliá tsánda** *an old bag* (fem.)
>
> το παλιό τραπέζι **to palió trapézi** *the old table* (neut.)

You can add **πολύ polí** *(very)* before the adjective, just like in English:

> Το σπίτι είναι πολύ μικρό.
> **to spíti íne polí mikró** *The house is very small.*
>
> Η τσάντα δεν είναι πολύ ακριβή.
> **i tsánda THen íne polí akriví** *The bag isn't very expensive.*
>
> Ο καφές είναι πολύ φτηνός.
> **o kafés íne polí ftinós** *The coffee is very inexpensive.*

Adjectival endings also change for the plural. You don't need to worry now about the detailed rules, but it's useful to know what is happening. Here are some examples:

> τα μικρά σπίτια **ta mikrá spítya** *the small houses*
>
> οι ακριβές τσάντες **i akrivés tsándes** *the expensive bags*

What does it mean?

Match the Greek with the pictures. Then read the Greek out loud and write the English next to each, as in the example.

ένα μεγάλο σάντουϊτς _____

ένα μικρό ποντίκι _____

ένας μικρός σκύλος _____*a small dog*_____

ένας καινούριος καναπές _____

ένα μεγάλο δέντρο _____

ένα πολύ παλιό αυτοκίνητο _____

ένα φτηνό κάδρο _____

ένας μικρός καφές _____

Listen and check

Listen to the conversation at the car rental company
and decide if these sentences are true or false.

24

		True	False
1	The conversation takes place in the evening	☐	☐
2	The woman wants to rent a car.	☐	☐
3	She thinks the first car is too expensive.	☐	☐
4	She thinks the second car is too big.	☐	☐
5	She likes the third car.	☐	☐

Unscramble the sentences

Look at the scrambled sentences below and write the correct order.

1 ένα/αυτοκίνητο/θέλω   ③ / ① / ②

2 είναι/το αυτοκίνητο/δεν/μεγάλο/πολύ   ☐ / ☐ / ☐ / ☐ / ☐

3 το αυτοκίνητο/ακριβό/είναι   ☐ / ☐ / ☐

4 το όνομά/Μαρία/μου/Βαζάκα/είναι   ☐ / ☐ / ☐ / ☐ / ☐

5 εγώ/την Αθήνα/από/είμαι   ☐ / ☐ / ☐ / ☐

Language Focus

To talk about what you and other people have, the most useful phrases are Έχω **ého** *(I have)*, έχει **éhi** *(he/she/it has)*, and έχουμε **éhoome** *(we have)*:

> Έχω έναν μεγάλο σκύλο.
> **ého énan megalo skílo**
> *I have a big dog.*
>
> Αυτός έχει ένα παλιό σπίτι στο Λονδίνο.
> **aftós éhi ena palió spíti sto lonτhíno**
> *He has an old house in London.*
>
> Έχουμε ένα καινούριο αυτοκίνητο.
> **éhoume ena kenoório aftokínito**
> *We have a new car.*

You could also ask Έχετε...; **éhete...?** *(Do you have...?)*:

> Έχετε ένα φτηνό αυτοκίνητο;
> **éhete éna ftinó aftokínito?**
> *Do you have an inexpensive car?*
>
> Έχετε ένα στιλό;
> **éhete éna stiló?**
> *Do you have a pen?*

25 Now you can take part in a conversation with the car rental company. Follow the prompts on your audio CD.

Key Words

το πόδι	**pódhi**	leg	το κεφάλι	**to kefáli**	head
το χέρι	**héri**	arm	η μύτη	**i míti**	nose
τα μάτια	**ta mátia**	eyes	το στόμα	**to stóma**	mouth
τα αυτιά	**ta aftiá**	ears	το στομάχι	**to stomáhi**	stomach
τα μαλλιά	**ta maliá**	hair	η ουρά	**i oorá**	tail

NOTE: **τα ta** means "the" when referring to neuter plural words.

By now you're probably feeling much more confident about reading and speaking Greek. Maybe you'd like to try writing the Greek letters for yourself. Although it's fun to copy and key the letters, you will need a guide to writing Greek in order to make sure you are forming them correctly. Handwritten Greek can also look significantly different from printed. (See page 89 for the Greek script and alphabet.)

Which word?

Circle the correct word to match the translation, as in the example.

1	head	πόλη	(κεφάλι)	καρέκλα	κρεβάτι
2	leg	δέντρο	αυτός	αργός	πόδι
3	stomach	σκύλος	γάτα·	καφές	στομάχι
4	mouth	στόμα	πού	στιλό	ντουλάπι
5	tail	βιβλίο	σπίτι	ουρά	δωμάτιο
6	hair	ποντίκι	μικρός	κάδρα	μαλλιά
7	ears	αυτή	αυτιά	είναι	τσάντα
8	nose	μύτη	από	εγώ	γρήγορος
9	eyes	είμαι	μάτια	ψυγείο	παλιός
10	arm	παλιός	έχει	χέρι	τραπέζι

At the circus

Can you use the words in the box to complete the description of the clowns, Carlos and Carlotta?

1 μεγάλο

2 μεγάλη

3 μικρή

4 παλιά

5 μικρό

6 μικρά

Ο Κάρλος έχει _____ μάτια και ένα _____ στομάχι.

Έχει μια _____ τσάντα στο χέρι.

Η Καρλόττα έχει μια _____ μύτη και ένα _____ στόμα.

Έχει μια _____ γάτα.

What does he look like?

What does the creature look like? Make as many sentences as you can describing what he looks like.

We've included some extra vocabulary you could use in your description.

Example:

Αυτός έχει ένα χοντρό στομάχι.
aftós éhi éna hondró stomáhi
He has a fat stomach.

beautiful	**όμορφος/-η/-ο**	ómorfos/-i/-o
ugly	**άσκημος/-η/-ο**	áskimos/-i/-o
fat	**χοντρός/-ή/-ό**	hondrós/-í/-ó
thin	**λεπτός/-ή/-ο**	leptós/-í/-ó
long	**μακρύς/-ιά/-ύ**	makrís/-yá/-í
short	**κοντός/-ή/-ό**	kondós/-í/-ó
strange	**παράξενος/-η/-ο**	paráksenos/-i/-o
wings	**φτερά**	fterá

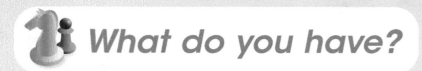

What do you have?

1. Cut out the picture cards from Game Card 5 and put them in a bag.

2. Cut out set 2 adjective cards and put them in a different bag.

3. Pull out one card from each bag without looking.

4. Make a sentence to match the cards you have chosen, for example:

   Εχω ένα παλιό κομπιούτερ.
   ého éna palió kompiúter
   I have an old computer.

5. Keep playing until all the cards have been chosen.

6. You can put the cards back in the bag and start again – each time the sentences will be different.

GAME CARD 5 (see page 53)

Picture cards:

Adjective cards:

μεγάλος	μικρός	καινούριος	παλιός
ακριβός	φτηνός	αργός	γρήγορος
όμορφος	άσκημος	παράξενος	μακρύς

παλιός

Key Words

το αεροδρόμιο	airport		**η γέφυρα** i yéfira	bridge
to aeroтнrómio (pl. **αεροδρόμια**)			(pl. **γέφυρες**)	
το σχολείο to skolío	school		**ο δρόμος** o тнrómos	street
(pl. **σχολεία**)			(pl. **δρόμοι**)	
το ξενοδοχείο	hotel		**το μουσείο** to moosío	museum
to ksenoтнohío (pl. **ξενοδοχεία**)			(pl. **μουσεία**)	
η τράπεζα i trápeza	bank		**το νοσοκομείο**	hospital
(pl. **τράπεζες**)			to nosokomío (pl. **νοσοκομεία**)	
το εστιατόριο	restaurant		**η στάση** i stási	bus stop
to estiatório (pl. **εστιατόρια**)			(pl. **στάσεις**)	
			πού...; poo?	where?
ο σταθμός o stathmós	station			
(pl. **σταθμοί**)			**κοντά σε** kondá se	near
το πάρκο to párko	park		**απεναντί από**	opposite
(pl. **πάρκα**)			apénandi apó	

You are new in town and are asking a Greek friend about the facilities. Follow the prompts on your audio CD.

28

Language Focus

Modern Greek has many loan words from other languages, particularly English, but also French. Some examples of these are **κομπιούτερ kompiúter** (*computer*), **ασανσέρ asansér** (*elevator*, from the French "ascenseur"), **σάντουϊτς sandouits** (*sandwich*).

In many cases, the English word itself derives from ancient Greek and then comes back into the language later! Some examples of this are: **τηλέφωνο tiléfono** telephone (literally "far voice"); **γεωγραφία yeografía** *geography* (literally "world drawing"). Think of "politics" – that comes from **πολιτική politikí** – something that relates to the word "city" (**πόλη póli**).

Questions and answers

Match the questions with their answers, as in the example.

Πού είναι η τράπεζα;	Το νοσοκομείο είναι κοντά στο σχολείο.
Υπάρχει ένα εστιατόριο;	Υπάρχει ένα ξενοδοχείο μπροστά από το σταθμό.
Υπάρχει ένα ξενοδοχείο;	Ναι, υπάρχει ένα εστιατόριο.
Πού είναι το νοσοκομείο;	Η γέφυρα είναι εκεί.
Πού είναι η γέφυρα;	Η τράπεζα είναι δίπλα στο σχολείο.

Key Words

29

το ταξί **to taksí**   *taxi*

(pl. ταξί)

το αεροπλάνο   *plane*

to aeropláno (pl. αεροπλάνα)

το λεωφορείο   *bus*

to leoforío (pl. λεωφορεία)

το ποδήλατο   *bicycle*

to poᴛʜílato (pl. ποδήλατα)

το τρένο **to tréno**   *train*

(pl. τρένα)

το πλοίο **to plío**   *boat*

(pl. πλοία)

Language Focus

To express how you travel, use **με me**, meaning "with," but you have to insert the word for "the" before the means of transport:

με το λεωφορείο **me to leoforío**   *by bus*

με το τρένο **me to tréno**   *by train*

με το αεροπλάνο **me to aeropláno**   *by plane*

με το πλοίο **me to plío**   *by boat*

με τα πόδια **me ta póᴛʜia**   *on foot (literally, "with the feet")*

Word Square

Can you find the seven different means of transportation in the word square?
Write out the pronunciation and meaning for the words you have found, as in
the example.

α	λ	υ	κ	η	τ	υ	ν	α
κ	ε	τ	α	μ	σ	η	α	υ
υ	ω	τ	α	ξ	ί	σ	ε	τ
η	φ	ρ	ξ	ρ	ε	δ	ρ	ο
π	ο	δ	ή	λ	α	τ	ο	κ
ό	ρ	ν	ε	ι	τ	α	π	ί
δ	ε	ο	η	κ	ρ	ε	λ	ν
ι	ί	α	σ	λ	έ	τ	ά	η
τ	ο	η	υ	α	ν	ρ	ν	τ
λ	ε	ω	π	λ	ο	ί	ο	ο

taksi (taxi) _____

_____

_____

_____

_____

_____

_____

 *Language Focus*

You have seen that plurals of Greek nouns have different endings from the singular and need to be learnt individually. However, there are some general rules that may help you.

Some masculine words end in **-ος -os**. Plurals of these words end in **-οι -i**.

> ### Υπάρχουν σκύλοι στο πάρκο.
> **ipárhoon skíli sto párko**
> *There are dogs in the park.*

Some feminine words end in **-α –a**. Plurals of these words end in **-ες -es**.

> ### Υπάρχουν γάτες στο δωμάτιο.
> **ipárhoon gátes sto THomátio**
> *There are cats in the room.*

Some neuter words end in **-ο –o**. Plurals of these words end in **-α -a**.

> ### Υπάρχουν βιβλία στο ντουλάπι.
> **ipárhoon vivlía sto doolápi**
> *There are books in the cupboard.*

The word for "the" also changes for plural words:

	As the subject	As the object
masc.	οι σκύλοι i skíli	τους σκύλους tous skílous *(the dogs)*
fem.	οι τσάντες i tsándes	τις τσάντες tis tsándes *(the bags)*
neuter	τα μάτια ta mátia	τα μάτια ta mátia *(the eyes)*

Key Words

συγνώμη	signómi	*excuse me!*
πώς πάω στον/στην/στο...	pos pao ston/stin/sto...	*how do I get to ...?*
πηγαίνετε...	piyénete...	*go...*
στρίψτε...	stípste...	*turn...*
δεξιά	THeksiá	*right/on the right*
αριστερά	aristerái	*left/on the left*

ευθεία	efthía	*straight ahead*
πάρτε τον πρώτο δρόμο	párte ton próto THrómo	*take the first street*
πάρτε τον δεύτερο δρόμο	párte ton THéftero THrómo	*take the second street*
εδώ	eTHó	*here*
εκεί	ekí	*there*
μετά	metá	*then/after that*

Ask for directions to places around town. Follow the prompts on your audio CD.

Which way?

Make questions and answers, as in the example.

Συγνώμη. Πώς πάω στο σταθμό;
signómi. pos pao sto stathmó?
Excuse me, how do I get to the station?

Πάρτε τον πρώτο δρόμο αριστερά.
párte ton próto ΤΗrómo aristerá
Take the first street on the left.

1

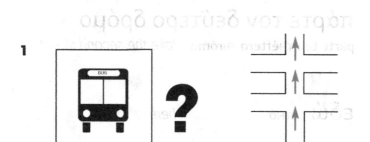

2

3

4

5

6

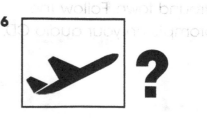

Around town

Below is a plan of a small town with some landmarks shown.
Starting from *You are here*, try to give directions to the following places:

ο σταθμός	το ξενοδοχείο Βύρωνας	το πάρκο	η στάση
o stathmós	**to ksenoτhohío Víronas**	**to párko**	**i stási**
the station	*the hotel Byron*	*the park*	*the bus stop*

For example, your directions to the station could be something like this:

Πηγαίνετε ευθεία από εδώ. Μετά, πάρτε τον πρώτο δρόμο δεξιά στην τράπεζα. Ο σταθμός είναι κοντά στην γέφυρα.

piyénete efthía apó eτhó. metá, párte ton próto τhrómo τheksiá stin trápeza. o stathmós íne kondá stin yéfira

Go straight ahead from here. After that, take the first street on the right at the bank. The station is near the bridge.

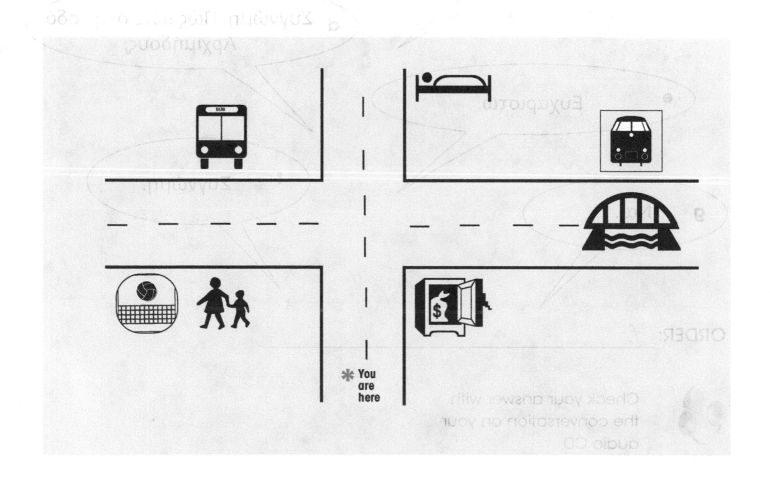

Unscramble the conversation

Put this conversation into the correct order.

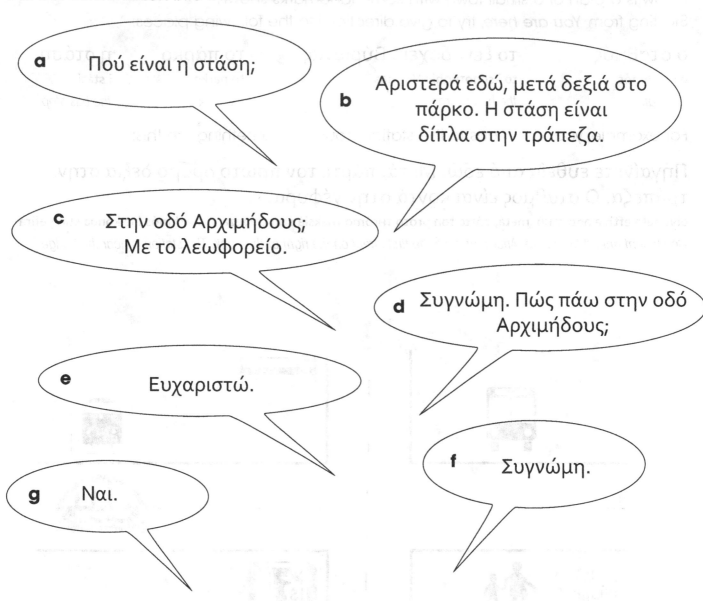

a Πού είναι η στάση;

b Αριστερά εδώ, μετά δεξιά στο πάρκο. Η στάση είναι δίπλα στην τράπεζα.

c Στην οδό Αρχιμήδους; Με το λεωφορείο.

d Συγνώμη. Πώς πάω στην οδό Αρχιμήδους;

e Ευχαριστώ.

f Συγνώμη.

g Ναι.

ORDER: _f,_ _____

Check your answer with the conversation on your audio CD.

32

Town Planning

33

1. Cut out the pictures of places around town from Game Card 6.

2. Listen to the first set of directions for the bank on your audio CD.

3. Pause the CD and stick the picture of the bank in the correct place on the town map on your game card.

4. Listen to the next set of directions and stick down the appropriate picture.

5. Repeat for all the directions until you have all your pictures stuck down on the map.

GAME CARD 6 (see page 63)
Picture cards:

You are here

6. Looking at the completed map, you could try to give directions to the various places yourself. For example:

Πάρτε τον δεύτερο δρόμο αριστερά.

Η τράπεζα είναι δεξιά, δίπλα στο σχολείο.

párte ton THéftero THrómo aristerá
i trápeza íne THeksiá, THípla sto skolío

(Take the second street on the left.
The bank is on the right, next to the school.)

You are here

Key Words

η γυναίκα **i yinéka**	wife	η κόρη **i kóri**	daughter	
		(pl. οι κόρες)		
ο άντρας **o ándras**	husband			
		ο γιός **o yiós**	son	
		(pl. οι αδελφές)		
η μητέρα **i mitéra**	mother			
		η αδελφή **i athelfí**	sister	
		(pl. οι αδελφές)		
ο πατέρας **o patéras**	father			
το παιδί **to pethí**	child	ο αδελφός **o athelfós**	brother	
(pl. τα παιδιά)		(pl. οι αδελφοί)		

 **Language Focus**

You saw the verb έχω **ého** (*I have*) earlier on page 48. You can also use this verb to talk about your family.

> Έχω μία αδελφή και έναν αδελφό.
> **ého mía athelfí ke énan athelfó**
> *I have a sister and a brother.*

To say what you *don't* have, you just insert the word δεν THen, meaning *not*, in front of the verb:

Δεν έχω μία αδελφή.
THen **ého mía athelfí**
I don't have a sister.

Δεν έχουμε παιδιά.
THen **éhoome pethiá**
We don't have children.

What does it mean?

Join the English to the pronunciation and the Greek script, as in the example.

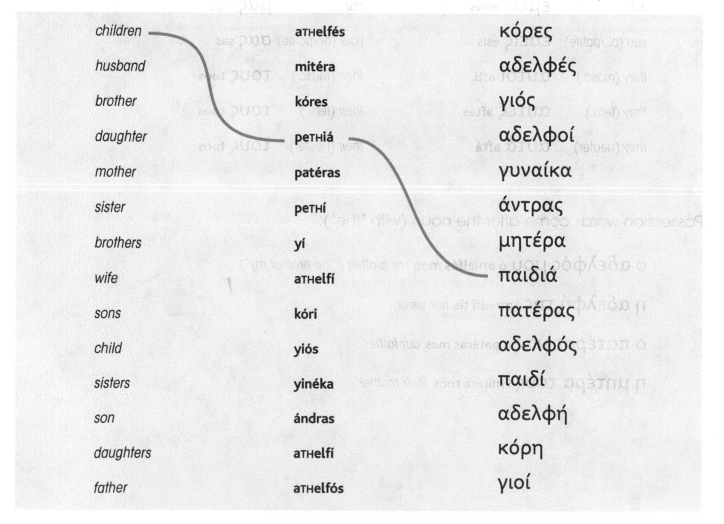

children	aTHelfés	κόρες
husband	mitéra	αδελφές
brother	kóres	γιός
daughter	peTHiá	αδελφοί
mother	patéras	γυναίκα
sister	peTHí	άντρας
brothers	yí	μητέρα
wife	aTHelfí	παιδιά
sons	kóri	πατέρας
child	yiós	αδελφός
sisters	yinéka	παιδί
son	ándras	αδελφή
daughters	aTHelfí	κόρη
father	aTHelfós	γιοί

Language Focus

You already know the words for *I*, *you*, *he*, and *she*, and how to say *my* and *your*. Here are the other pronouns and possessive words:

pronoun			possessive		
I	εγώ	egó	*my*	μου	moo
you (informal)	εσύ	esí	*your* (informal)	σου	soo
he	αυτός	aftós	*his*	του	too
she	αυτή	aftí	*her*	της	tis
it	αυτό	aftó	*its*	του	too
we	εμείς	emís	*our*	μας	mas
you (pl./polite)	εσείς	esís	*your* (pl./polite)	σας	sas
they (masc.)	αυτοί	aftí	*their* (masc.)	τους	toos
they (fem.)	αυτές	aftés	*their* (fem.)	τους	toos
they (neuter)	αυτά	aftá	*their* (neuter)	τους	toos

Possession words come after the noun (with "the"):

ο αδελφός μου **o aτHelfós moo** *my brother ("the brother my")*

η αδελφή της **i aτHelfí tis** *her sister*

ο πατέρας μας **o patéras mas** *our father*

η μητέρα τους **i mitéra toos** *their mother*

If you want to introduce someone, you can use the simple phrase **εδώ είναι ετнό íne** ("here is"). You need to add **o o** (masc.) or **η i** (fem.) before the name.

> ## Εδώ είναι ο αδελφός μου, ο Γιάννης.
> **ετнό íne o атнelfós moo, o Yiánnis**
> *This is my brother, Giannis. ["here is my brother, Giannis"]*
>
> ## Εδώ είναι η αδελφή μου, η Άννα.
> **ετнó íne i атнelfí moo, i Anna**
> *This is my sister, Anna. ["here is my sister, Anna"]*

Family Tree

Look at the family tree and imagine you are one of the members of the family. Make up sentences about your relatives, as in the example.

Εδώ είναι η κόρη μου, η Ελένη.
ετнó íne i kóri moo, i Eléni
This is my daughter, Eleni.

Γιάννης Άννα

Παύλος Ελένη

Giorgos's family

Listen to Giorgos answering questions about his family.
Circle the correct names on the family tree, as in the example.

35

Παύλος
Κώστας
Γιώργος

Αντρέα
Ελένη
Μαρία

(Γιώργος)
Κώστας
Χάρρυ

Γιάννης
Παύλος
Κώστας

Questions and answers

Now read the questions on the left and then match them to the answers on the right that Giorgos gave, as in the example.

1 Έχεις αδελφούς;

2 Πώς είναι το όνομα της μητέρας σου;

3 Έχεις αδελφές;

4 Πώς είναι το όνομά του αδελφού σου;

5 Πώς είναι το όνομα του πατέρα σου;

6 Πώς είναι το όνομά σου;

7 Από πού είσαι;

a Το όνομά της είναι Μαρία.

b Όχι. Δεν έχω αδελφές.

c Το όνομά του είναι Κώστας.

d Είμαι από την Χαλκίδα.

e Το όνομά μου είναι Γιώργος.

f Το όνομά του είναι Παύλος.

g Ναι. Έχω έναν αδελφό.

 # Language Focus

Who? is Ποιός; piós?:

Ποιός είναι αυτός; piós íne aftós? *Who's this?*

Remember how to say *"pleased to meet you"* from Topic 1: χαίρω πολύ héro polí.

You can put all this together to make a short conversation:

— Γειά σου, Άννα.
yiásoo, Ánna
Hello, Anna.

— Γειά σου, Αντρέα. Ποιός είναι αυτός;
yiásoo, Andréa. piós íne aftós?
Hello, Andrea. Who's this?

— Εδώ είναι ο αδελφός μου, ο Γιάννης.
eτHό íne o aτHelfós moo, o Yiánnis
This is my brother, Gianni.

— Γειά σου, Γιάννη. Χαίρω πολύ.
yiásou, Yiánni. héro polí
Hello, Gianni. Pleased to meet you..

— Χαίρω πολύ, Αντρέα.
héro polí, Andréa
Pleased to meet you, Andrea.

Now introduce <u>your</u> family. Follow the prompts on your audio CD.

36

37

Key Words

ένα	éna	one	έξι	éksi	six
δύο	THío	two	εφτά	eftá	seven
τρία	tría	three	οχτώ	októ	eight
τέσσερα	téssera	four	εννέα	enéa	nine
πέντε	pénde	five	δέκα	THéka	ten

 ## Language Focus

Numbers in Greek have some special features to do with gender. As you know, the article *a/an* in Greek has three forms. The neuter form ένα éna is the same as the word for *one* when you are counting in general. However, if the person or thing you are counting is feminine or masculine, the word for *one* changes:

> Έχω μία αδελφή και έναν αδελφό.
> **ého mía aTHelfí ke énan aTHelfó**
> *I have one sister and and one brother.*

The word for *two* does not change in the same way, but *three* and *four* also change according to gender. *Three* is τρεις tris for feminine and masculine nouns but τρία tría for neuter nouns. *Four* is τέσσερις tésseris for feminine and masculine nouns, but τέσσερα téssera for neuter nouns:

> Έχω τρεις αδελφές και τρία παιδιά.
> **ého tris aTHelfés ke tría peTHiá**
> *I have three sisters and three children.*

> Έχουμε τέσσερις αδελφούς και τέσσερα παιδιά.
> **éhoome tésseris aTHelfoós ke téssera peTHiá**
> *We have four brothers and four children.*

How many?

Match the numbers with the figures, as in the example.

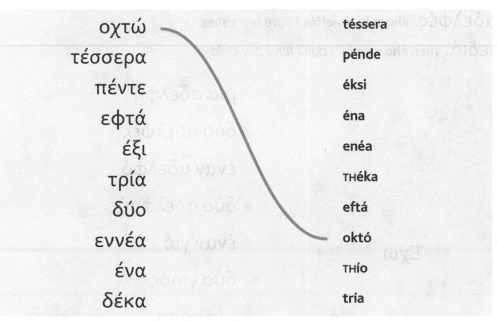

οχτώ	téssera
τέσσερα	pénde
πέντε	éksi
εφτά	éna
έξι	enéa
τρία	THéka
δύο	eftá
εννέα	októ
ένα	THío
δέκα	tría

Greek sums

Circle the correct answer to these sums, as in the example.

1 ένα + τρία =   ένα δύο τρία (τέσσερα) πέντε έξι εφτά οχτώ εννέα δέκα

2 έξι + δύο =   ένα δύο τρία τέσσερα πέντε έξι εφτά οχτώ εννέα δέκα

3 δύο + ένα =   ένα δύο τρία τέσσερα πέντε έξι εφτά οχτώ εννέα δέκα

4 εφτά + δύο =   ένα δύο τρία τέσσερα πέντε έξι εφτά οχτώ εννέα δέκα

5 δύο + πέντε =   ένα δύο τρία τέσσερα πέντε έξι εφτά οχτώ εννέα δέκα

6 τρία + τρία =   ένα δύο τρία τέσσερα πέντε έξι εφτά οχτώ εννέα δέκα

7 οχτώ + δύο =   ένα δύο τρία τέσσερα πέντε έξι εφτά οχτώ εννέα δέκα

8 έξι + τρία =   ένα δύο τρία τέσσερα πέντε έξι εφτά οχτώ εννέα δέκα

9 ένα + εννέα =   ένα δύο τρία τέσσερα πέντε έξι εφτά οχτώ εννέα δέκα

My family

Use the table below to make sentences about yourself, as in the examples.

Έχω δύο αδελφές. ého THío aτHelfés *I have two sisters.*

Δεν έχω πεδιά. THen ého peτHia *I don't have any children.*

	μία αδελφή
	δύο αδελφές
	έναν αδελφό
	δύο αδελφούς
Έχω	έναν γιό
	δύο γιούς
	μία κόρη
	δύο κόρες
	ένα παιδί
	δύο παιδιά

Listen and speak

Now imagine you are with some of your family looking for the station and you meet a Greek friend.   **38**

Carefully prepare the information below that you will need to take part in the conversation. Then go to your audio CD and see how you get on introducing your family.

1 Think of two members of your family – one male and one female. For example, your husband and your daughter; or your brother and your mother.

2 How would you tell someone their names in Greek?

3 How would you ask *How do I get to the station?*

4 How do you say *thank you* and *goodbye*?

You can repeat the conversation, but this time use two different members of your family and ask how to get to the bus stop.

Bingo!

1. Cut out the small number tokens and the bingo cards on Game Card 7.

2. Find 16 buttons for each player or make 16 small blank pieces of card (to cover the squares on the bingo card).

3. Put the tokens into a bag and shake thoroughly.

4. Pull out a number token and say the number out loud in Greek.

5. If you have that number on your card, cover the square with a button or blank piece of card. If you have more than one square with that number, you can only cover one.

6. Put the number token back in the bag and shake again.

7. Repeat steps 3–6 until you have all the squares covered on the bingo card. Then you can shout:

   Νίκησα! **níkisa** I've won!

   You can play with a friend or challenge yourself.

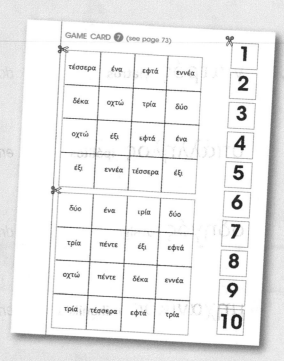

GAME CARD 7 (see page 73)

τέσσερα	ένα	εφτά	εννέα
δέκα	οχτώ	τρία	δύο
οχτώ	έξι	εφτά	ένα
έξι	εννέα	τέσσερα	έξι

δύο	ένα	τρία	δύο
τρία	πέντε	έξι	εφτά
οχτώ	πέντε	δέκα	εννέα
τρία	τέσσερα	εφτά	τρία

1 2 3 4 5 6 7 8 9 10

δύο	ένα	τρία	δύο
	πέντε	έξι	εφτά
οχτώ	πέντε		εννέα
τρία	τέσσερα	εφτά	τρία

 **Key Words**

γιατρός yiatrós	doctor	μάγειρας máyiras — cook/chef
		(fem. μαγείρισσα mayírisa)
υπάλληλος ipálilos	employee	
		λογιστής loyistís — accountant
οδηγός οΤΗigós	driver	(fem. λογίστρια loyístria)
μηχανικός mihanikós	engineer	δάσκαλος ΤΗáskalos — teacher
		(fem. δασκάλα ΤΗáskala)
ηθοποιός ithopiós	actor	
		φοιτητής fititís — student
δικηγόρος ΤΗikigóros	lawyer	(fem. φοιτήτρια fitítria)

Notice that some jobs have a different ending for the feminine, but others use the same word for both males and females.

If your job or those of your family aren't listed here, try to find out what they are in Greek.

What does it mean?

Join the Greek to the pronunciation and the English, as in the example.

Greek	Pronunciation	English
δάσκαλος	οτΗigós	*employee*
φοιτητής	ithopiós	*accountant*
γιατρός	τΗikigóros	*actor*
μάγειρας	yiatrós	*driver*
υπάλληλος	máyiras	*lawyer*
μηχανικός	τΗáskalos	*engineer*
λογιστής	fititís	*doctor*
οδηγός	ipálilos	*cook/chef*
ηθοποιός	mihanikós	*teacher*
δικηγόρος	loyistís	*student*

The tools of the trade

Match the jobs to the tools of the trade, as in the example.

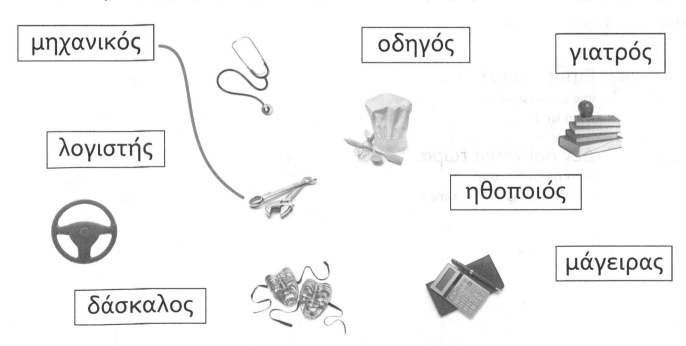

μηχανικός

οδηγός

γιατρός

λογιστής

ηθοποιός

δάσκαλος

μάγειρας

Language Focus

To ask what someone does for a living, you use the phrase:

Τι δουλειά κάνετε; ti THooliá kánete *What work do you do?*

You will have noticed on page 75 that some professions have a different male and female form of the word, and the answer will vary accordingly:

> **Τι δουλειά κάνετε; ti THooliá kánete?**
> *What work do you do?*
>
> **Είμαι γιατρός. íme yiatrós** *I am [a] doctor. (male or female)*
>
> **Τι δουλειά κάνετε; ti THouliá kánete?**
> *What work do you do?*
>
> **Είμαι μάγειρας. íme máyiras** *I am [a] cook. (male)*
>
> **Τι δουλειά κάνετε; ti THouliá kánete?**
> *What work do you do?*
>
> **Είμαι δασκάλα. íme THaskála** *I am [a] teacher. (female)*

Notice that you do not need the word for "a" in Greek in this expression.

Other possible answers include:

> **Είμαι συνταξιούχος.**
> **íme sindaksioóhos**
> *I'm retired.*
>
> **Δεν δουλεύω τώρα.**
> **THen THoolévo tóra**
> *I'm not working at the moment.*

Listen and note

Listen to two people telling you about themselves
and fill out the details in English on the forms below.

40

Name: *Maria*

Family name: ....

Nationality: ....

Name of spouse: ....

No. of children: ....

Occupation: ....

Name: ....

Family name: ....

Nationality: ....

Name of spouse: ....

No. of children: ....

Occupation: ....

Your turn to speak

Now you give same information about yourself.
Follow the prompts on your audio CD.

41

What's the answer?

Match the questions to the answers.

For example: **1d**

1 Πώς είναι το όνομά σας;

2 Από πού είστε;

3 Πώς είναι το όνομα της γυναίκας σας;

4 Έχετε παιδιά;

5 Τι δουλειά κάνετε;

6 Πώς είναι το όνομα του γιού σας;

a Ναι, έχω ένα γιό και δύο κόρες.

b Είμαι ηθοποιός.

c Είμαι από την Αυστραλία.

d Το όνομά μου είναι Χάρι.

e Το όνομά της είναι Τζαστήν.

f Το όνομά του είναι Σάμι.

Which word?

Write the correct number of the word in the box to complete the description, as in the example.

1 γυναίκας **2** γιό

3 ηθοποιός **4** κόρες

5 παιδιά

Το όνομά μου είναι Χάρι και είμαι ___3___ . Είμαι από την Μελβούρνη στην Αυστραλία.

Το όνομα της _____ μου είναι Τζαστήν, και έχω τρία _____:

ένα _____ και δύο _____ .

 **Key Words**

42

το εργοστάσιο	*factory*	το γραφείο	*office*
ergostásio (pl. εργοστάσια)		**grafío** (pl. γραφεία)	
το κατάστημα	*store*	το πανεπιστήμιο	*university*
katastima (pl. καταστήματα)		**panepistímio** (pl. πανεπιστήμια)	
το θέατρο	*theater*	η εταιρία·	*company/*
théatro (pl. θέατρα)		**etería** (pl. εταιρίες)	*business*

See page 54 for more places to work.

 Language Focus

To answer the question Πού δουλεύετε; **poo тноolévete** *Where do you work?*
you can use the phrase Δουλεύω σε... **тноolévo se...** *I work in...* :

> Είμαι γιατρός και δουλεύω σε ένα μικρό
> νοσοκομείο στην Θεσσαλονίκη.
> **íme yiatrós ke тноolévo se éna mikró nosokomío stin thesaloníki**
> *I am a doctor and I work in a small hospital in Thessaloniki.*
>
> Δουλεύω σε μία μεγάλη εταιρία στην Αθήνα.
> **тноolévo se mía megáli etería stin athína**
> *I work in a large company in Athens.*

Where do I work?

Can you match the work places to the jobs, as in the example?

μηχανικός	τράπεζα
δάσκαλος	εστιατόριο
ηθοποιός	εργοστάσιο
υπάλληλος	σχολείο
λογιστής	νοσοκομείο
μάγειρας	γραφείο
γιατρός	θέατρο

Now make sentences for each of the work places, as in the example:

Είμαι μηχανικός και δουλεύω σε ένα εργοστάσιο.
íme mihanikós ke тноolévo **se éna ergostásio**
I'm an engineer and I work in a factory.

What are they saying?

Match the people with what they are saying. For example: **1d**

1 Δουλεύω σε ένα σχολείο στην Αγγλία.

2 Δουλεύω σε ένα εστιατόριο στην Αθήνα.

3 Δουλεύω σε μία αμερικανική τράπεζα.

4 Δουλεύω σε ένα κατάστημα στην Θεσσαλονίκη.

5 Δουλεύω σε ένα θέατρο στην Ιρλανδία.

6 Δουλεύω σε ένα εργοστάσιο στον Καναδά.

a

b

c

d

e

f

TOPIC 8

Listen and speak

43

Imagine you are a chef. You're meeting someone for the first time and they are asking you about yourself.

Carefully prepare the information below that you will need to take part in the conversation. Then go to your audio CD and see how you get on talking about yourself.

1 Your name is Giannis Leonidas (Γιάννης Λεωνίδας).

2 You're from Athens, Greece but you work in America.

3 You're a chef.

4 You work in a Greek restaurant in New York.

5 You have two daughters.

6 Your wife is a teacher in a big school.

Which word?

Now write the correct number of the word in the box to complete the description of Minoru's life, as in the example.

1 ελληνικό	**2** πανεπιστήμιο	**3** μάγειρας	**4** εστιατόριο
5 δασκάλα	**6** φοιτήτριες	**7** σχολείο	**8** δουλεύω

Το όνομά μου είναι Γιάννης Λεωνίδας. Είμαι __*3*__ . Είμαι από

την Αθήνα στην Ελλάδα, αλλά _____ σε ένα _____ _____

στην Νέα Υόρκη. Η γυναίκα μου είναι _____ και δουλεύει σε ένα

μεγάλο _____ κοντά στο εστιατόριο. Έχουμε δύο κόρες και

είναι _____ στο _____ .

Where do I work?

1. Tear out the work-place picture cards and profession word cards on Game Card 8.

2. Turn the cards face down on a table, with the pictures on one end of the table and the words on the other.

3. Turn a word card and say Είμαι... íme..., not forgetting to change the ending to the feminine if you are female, for example:

   Είμαι δάσκαλος/δασκάλα.
   íme THáskalos/THaskála *I'm a teacher.*

4. Then turn over a picture card. If the work-place picture matches the profession, say Δουλεύω σε ένα/μία... THoolévo se éna/mía..., for example:

   Δουλεύω σε ένα σχολείο.
   THoolévo se éna skolío *I work in a school.*

5. If you turn over a matching picture and say both sentences correctly you get to keep the cards. If you don't, you must turn the cards face down and try again.

6. The winner is the one who collects the most cards.

7. You can compete with a friend or challenge yourself against the clock.

(Review the vocabulary on pages 54, 56 and 74 before you play the game.)

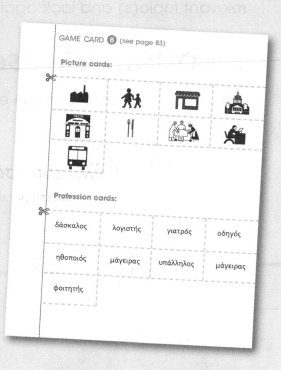

GAME CARD 8 (see page 83)

Picture cards:

Profession cards:

δάσκαλος	λογιστής	γιατρός	οδηγός
ηθοποιός	μάγειρας	υπάλληλος	μάγειρας
φοιτητής			

δάσκαλος

TEST YOURSELF

This *Test Yourself* section reviews all the Greek you have learned in this program. Have a go at the activities. If you find you have forgotten something, go back to the relevant topic(s) and look again at the **Key Words** and **Language Focus** panels.

I want..., please.

Ask for the following, as in the example:

Θέλω ένα τσάϊ, παρακαλώ.

thélo ena tsai, parakaló

1

2

3

4

5

Listen and check

Listen to Katerina talking about herself and decide if the following sentences are true or false.

44

		True	False
1	Katerina is Greek.	☐	☐
2	She comes from a small town.	☐	☐
3	She's a teacher.	☐	☐
4	She works in England.	☐	☐
5	Her husband is an engineer.	☐	☐
6	She has five children.	☐	☐

Which word?

Now write the correct number of the word in the box to complete the description of Katerina, as in the example.

1 δίπλα	2 γιό	3 ελληνικό	4 τέσσερα
5 νοσοκομείο	6 πόλη	7 γιατρός	8 Ελλάδα

Το όνομά μου είναι Κατερίνα, και είμαι από την Θεσσαλονίκη, μία

μεγάλη __6__ στην ____ . Είμαι δασκάλα, και δουλεύω σε ένα μικρό

____ σχολείο στην Αγγλία. Ο άντρας μου είναι ____, και δουλεύει σε

ένα μεγάλο ____ ____ στο ελληνικό σχολείο. Έχουμε ____ παιδιά,

ένα ____ και τρεις κόρες.

Can you try and make up a similar description about yourself?

Read and check

Look at the picture and decide if the sentences are true or false. (For "left" and "right," imagine you have your back to the buildings.)
Look back at topics 4–6 if you are unsure of any of the words.

	True	False
1 Υπάρχει μία τράπεζα στο κάδρο.	☐	☐
2 Υπάρχει ένα νοσοκομείο δίπλα στην τράπεζα δεξιά.	☐	☐
3 Υπάρχει ένα σχολείο δίπλα στην τράπεζα αριστερά.	☐	☐
4 Υπάρχει ένας σκύλος στο δρόμο.	☐	☐
5 Δεν υπάρχουν αυτοκίνητα στο δρόμο.	☐	☐
6 Υπάρχει μία μικρή γάτα πάνω από το αυτοκίνητο.	☐	☐
7 Υπάρχουν μεγάλα δέντρα πίσω από το σχολείο.	☐	☐
8 Υπάρχει ένα παλιό ποδήλατο μπροστά από το νοσοκομείο.	☐	☐

What does it mean?

Can you remember these words? Join the words and write the pronunciation next to the Greek, as in the example.

children	γιός	*γιός*
husband	αδελφός	
son	γιοί	
daughter	κόρες	
father	παιδί	
mother	μητέρα	
brother	αδελφή	
daughters	γυναίκα	
child	αδελφοί	
wife	παιδιά	
sister	άντρας	
brothers	αδελφές	
sons	κόρη	
sisters	πατέρας	

How do you say it?

Now see if you can say these in Greek, as in the example.

1 My husband is a doctor.
Ο άντρας μου είναι γιατρός.
o ándras moo íne yiatrós

2 I have four children.

3 His son is an engineer.

4 Maria's mother is from Athens.

5 My wife's name is Claire.

6 My brother is an actor.

7 I don't have any sisters.

8 I have three daughters.

At the tourist office

45

Finally, you are going to test your new Greek conversational skills by joining in the dialog on your audio CD.

You're going to ask for some information at a tourist information office.

To prepare, first see if you can remember these words and phrases. Write the pronunciation and English next to the Greek, as in the example.

αντίο	*adio goodbye*
ευχαριστώ	
πίσω από	
δεξιά	
αριστερά	
δρόμος	
λεωφορείο	
κοντά	
μεγάλος/-η/-ο	
μουσείο	
πού	
καλημέρα	

Now follow the prompts on your audio CD. Don't worry if you don't manage everything the first time around. Just keep repeating it until you are fluent.

Congratulations on successfully completing this introductory *Read & Speak Greek* program. You have overcome the obstacle of learning an unfamiliar language and a different script. You should now have the confidence to enjoy using the Greek you have learned. You have also acquired a sound basis from which to expand your language skills in whichever direction you choose. Good luck!

This *Reference* section gives an overview of the Greek script and pronunciation. You can use it to refer to as you work your way through the *Read & Speak Greek* program. Don't expect to take it all in from the beginning. *Read & Speak Greek* is designed to build your confidence step by step as you progress through the topics. The details will start to fall into place gradually as you become more familiar with the Greek letters and language.

The Greek script

The Greek script is not nearly as difficult as it might seem at first glance. There are many letters that are the same as the English ones, there are capital letters, and, unlike English, words are usually spelled as they sound.

There are 24 letters altogether in the Greek alphabet. A good way of remembering the alphabet is to divide the letters into three groups.

The first group consists of ten letters which look and sound like their English equivalents. Eight are very similar – but watch out for lower case Z (ζ) and M (μ):

Capital letter:	A	E	Z	I	K	M	O	T
Lower case:	α	ε	ζ	ι	κ	μ	ο	τ
Pronunciation:	a	e	z	i	k	m	o	t

The other letters in this group can be misleading. The Greek N n is pronounced the same as English but in lower case looks like an English "v." Likewise the Greek Y i looks like an English "u" in lower case (see also page 91 for pronunciation):

Capital letter:	N	Y
Lower case:	ν	υ
Pronunciation:	n	i

The second group of letters resemble English letters as capitals, but they represent totally different sounds. These are called "false friends."

Capital letter:	B	H	P	Γ	X
Lower case:	β	η	ρ	γ	χ
Pronunciation:	v	i	r	g/y	h (hard)

The third group consists of the remaining nine letters that have unfamiliar shapes, although most of them represent sounds familiar to an English-speaker. The first four shown below represent sounds that in English are made by putting two letters together. Some of these letters may look familiar through their use in mathematics and science.

Capital letter:	Δ	Θ	Ξ	Ψ	Φ	Λ	Π	Σ	Ω
Lower case:	δ	θ	ξ	ψ	φ	λ	π	σ, ς*	ω
Pronunciation:	TH	th	ks	ps	f	l	p	s	o

* The form of this letter depends on its position in a word.
ς is only used at the end of a word, otherwise σ is used,
e.g. σκύλος skilos – *dog*.

The Greek alphabet

The table below shows all the Greek letters, both capitals and lower case, in alphabetical order with their pronunciation. You can refer to it as you work your way through the topics.

A	α	a	I	ι	i	P	ρ	r
B	β	v	K	κ	k	Σ	σ/ς	s
Γ	γ	gh or y	Λ	λ	l	T	τ	t
Δ	δ	TH (as in "that")	M	μ	m	Y	υ	i
E	ε	e	N	ν	n	Φ	φ	f
Z	ζ	z	Ξ	ξ	ks	X	χ	h
H	η	i	O	o	o	Ψ	ψ	ps
Θ	θ	th (as in "thin")	Π	π	p	Ω	ω	o

Pronunciation

Greek is probably one of the easiest languages to read as what you see is generally what you hear. The Greek used today is very much simplified. The once prolific stress and breathing marks have been reduced to only one small accent above a vowel (e.g. ό) which indicates where the stress falls on a word.

The Greek vowels have simple pronunciations:

Α/α	always pronounced "a" as in "bat"
Ε/ε	always pronounced "e" as in "bed"
Ι/ι, Υ/υ, Η/η	all pronounced "ee" as in "feet"
Ο/ο, Ω/ω	both pronounced "o" as in "pot

A combination of two vowels may produce a different sound. Use the pronunciation guide for individual words to help you. Note these

αυ	pronounced "af" or "av", e.g. . αυτοκίνητο **aftokínito** – "car"; Παύλος **pávlos**
ευ	pronounced "ef" or "ev", e.g. ευχαριστώ **efharistó** – "thank you"

Many of the other Greek letters are pronounced in a similar way to their English equivalents, but here are a few points to note:

Ρ/ρ (r)	pronounced trilled as the Scottish "r" at of the front of the mouth
Χ/χ (h)	pronounced like the "ch" in the Yiddish "chutzpah"
Γ/γ (gh or y)	pronounced like a softer "g," except when it is followed by an i or e sound, when it is pronounced as "y" in the English "yes."

You will find an introduction to the sounds of Greek on track 1 of your audio.

ANSWERS

Topic 1

Page 6

Check your answers with the Key Words panel on page 5.

Page 8: What are they saying?

Page 8: What do you hear?

You should have checked boxes 2 and 5.

Page 10: What does it mean?

1d, 2f, 3e, 4b, 5a, 6c

Page 10: Which word?

Καλη _____2_____.

Γειά σας, _____5_____ σπέρα.

Το _____4_____ μου _____6_____ Άννα.

Πως είναι το όνομά _____3_____;

Το όνομά _____1_____ είναι Γιώργος.

Page 11: What are their names?

Κάθριν	Catherine	Τζων	John
Μαίρη	Mary	Ντέϊβιντ	David
Ανν	Ann	Μάϊκλ	Michael
Ελίζαμπεθ	Elizabeth	Χάρρυ	Harry

Page 12: In or out?

IN: Elizabeth, John, Harry, Catherine, David

OUT: Anna, Kostas, Michael, Yiorgos, Mary

Topic 2

Page 15: Where are the countries?

ο Καναδάς 1	η Ελλάδα 6	η Αγγλία 4
η Ιταλία 5	η Ιρλανδία 3	η Αμερική 2
η Τουρκία 7	η Αυστραλία 8	

Page 16: How do you say it?

Check your answers with the Key Words panel on page 14.

Page 16: Where are the cities?

Η Αθήνα είναι στην Ελλάδα. **i athína íne stin eláτha**

Η Νέα Υόρκη είναι στην Αμερική. **i nea yórki íne stin amerikí**

Το Ουάσινγκτον είναι στην Αμερική. **i ouásington íne stin amerikí**

Η Αγκύρα είναι στην Τουρκία. **i ángira íne stin tourkía**

Η Θεσσαλονίκη είναι στην Ελλάδα. **i thessaloníki íne stin eláτha**

Το Σίντνεϊ είναι στην Αυστραλία. **to sídnei íne stin avstralía**

Το Λονδίνο είναι στην Αγγλία. **to lonτhíno íne stin anglía**

Το Δουβλίνο είναι στην Ιρλανδία. **to τhoovlíno íne stin irlanτhía**

Page 17: Audio track 8

Maria: Greece; Michael: America; Susan: England; Selim: Turkey; Nicoletta: Italy; Stuart: Canada

Page 18: Where are they from?

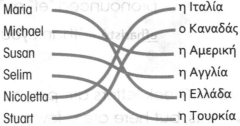

Maria — η Ιταλία
Michael — ο Καναδάς
Susan — η Αμερική
Selim — η Αγγλία
Nicoletta — η Ελλάδα
Stuart — η Τουρκία

Page 20: Who's from where?

1 Αυτός είναι από την Νέα Υόρκη, στην Αμερική.
aftós íne apó tin néa yórki, stin amerikí.

2 Αυτή είναι από την Αθήνα, στην Ελλάδα.
aftí íne apó tin athína stin eláτha.

3 Αυτή είναι από το Βανκούβερ, στον Καναδά.
aftí íne apó to vankoúver, ston kanaτhá

4 Αυτός είναι από το Σίντνεϊ, στην Αυστραλία.
aftós íne apó to sídnei, stin afstralía

5 Αυτός είναι από το Δουβλίνο, στην Ιρλανδία.
aftós íne apó to τhoovlíno, stin irlanτhía

6 Αυτή είναι από την Ρώμη, στην Ιταλία.
aftí íne apó tin rómi, stin italía

7 Αυτός είναι από την Αγκύρα, στην Τουρκία.
  aftós íne apó tin angíra, stin tourkía

8 Αυτή είναι από το Λονδίνο, στην Αγγλία.
  aftí íne apó to lontнíno, stin anglía

Page 21: Listen and Check

1 False; **2** True; **3** False; **4** True; **5** False

Page 21: What does it mean?

I'm from Canada. — Το όνομά μου είναι Λούσυ.

He's from Greece. — Εγώ είμαι από τον Καναδά.

My name's Lucy. — Γειά σας.

What's your name? — Πώς είναι το όνομά σας;

Good evening. — Αυτός είναι από την Ελλάδα.

Hello. — Καλησπέρα

Page 22: What does it mean?

1 Το όνομά μου είναι Λούσυ. My name is Lucy.

2 Είμαι από τον Καναδά. I'm Canadian.

3 Ο Κώστας είναι από την Ελλάδα. Kostas is from Greece.

4 Πώς είναι το όνομά σας; What's your name?

5 Το όνομά μου είναι Μαρία. My name is Maria.

6 Από πού είναι αυτός; Where is he from?

7 Αυτός είναι από την Αγγλία. He's from England.

8 Αυτή είναι από την Αμερική. She's from America.

Topic 3

Page 25

Check your answers with the Key Words panel on page 24.

Page 26: Word Square

sofa, table, book, door, chair, telephone, bag

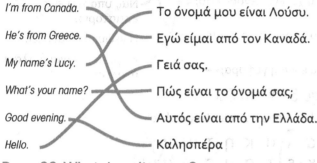

Page 26: Odd One Out

κομπιούτερ * παράθυρο * (καλημέρα) * τηλεόραση

(η πόρτα) * η Ελλάδα * η Αμερική * η Αγγλία

βιβλίο * (όνομα) * περιοδικό * στιλό

(πόλη) * καναπές * καρέκλα * τραπέζι

καλησπέρα * γειά σας * καλημέρα * (καρέκλα)

Page 28: What's this?

1e, 2b, 3f, 4c, 5a, 6d, 7h, 8g

Page 30: Who orders what?

Customer 1: coffee & sandwich; **Customer 2:** coffee & cake; **Customer 3:** coffee & sweet; **Customer 4:** tea, cake & ice cream; **Customer 5:** tea, coffee and cheese pie

Page 31: Unscramble the conversation

g, a, e, c, f, h, d, b

Topic 4

Page 35: What does it mean?

Check your answers with the Key Words panel on page 34.

Page 35: What can you see?

γάτα ☑	ψυγείο ☐
σκύλος ☐	παράθυρο ☑
φούρνος ☐	κρεβάτι ☑
τραπέζι ☑	κουρτίνα ☑
στιλό ☑	ποντίκι ☐
βιβλίο ☑	πόρτα ☐
περιοδικό ☐	κάδρο ☑
κομπιούτερ ☑	ντουλάπι ☐
τσάντα ☑	καρέκλα ☑

Page 37: Which word?

1 μπροστά από **2** κάτω από **3** πάνω από **4** σ(ε)

5 κάτω από **6** δίπλα σ(ε) **7** μέσα σ(ε)

Answers

Page 39: Where are the mice?

There are many possible sentences.

If you can, check yours with a native speaker.

Page 41: True or False?

1 True; 2 False; 3 False; 4 False; 5 False; 6 True; 7 False;
8 True; 9 True 10 True

Topic 5

Page 44: Can you remember?

Check your answers with the Key Words panel on page 44.

Page 46: What does it mean?

ένα μεγάλο σάντουϊτς	a big sandwich
ένα μικρό ποντίκι	a small mouse
ένας μικρός σκύλος	a small dog
ένας καινούριος καναπές	a new sofa
ένα μεγάλο δέντρο	a big tree
ένα πολύ παλιό αυτοκίνητο	a very old car
ένα φτηνό κάδρο	an inexpensive picture
ένας μικρός καφές	a small coffee

Page 47: Listen and check

1 False; 2 True; 3 True; 4 False; 5 True

Page 47: Unscramble the sentences

1 312   2 23154   3 132   4 13524   5 1432

Page 50: Which word?

1 κεφάλι 2 πόδι 3 στομάχι 4 στόμα 5 ουρά

6 μαλλιά 7 αυτιά 8 μύτη 9 μάτια 10 χέρι

Page 51: At the circus

Ο Κάρλος έχει 6 μάτια και ένα 1 στομάχι.

Έχει μια 4 τσάντα στο χέρι.

Η Καρλόττα έχει μια 2 μύτη και ένα 5 στόμα.

Έχει μια 3 γάτα.

Page 52: What does it look like?

There are many possible sentences.

If you can, check yours with a native speaker.

Topic 6

Page 55: Questions and answers

Πού είναι η τράπεζα;

Υπάρχει ένα εστιατόριο;

Υπάρχει ένα ξενοδοχείο;

Πού είναι το νοσοκομείο;

Πού είναι η γέφυρα;

Το νοσοκομείο είναι κοντά στο σχολείο.

Υπάρχει ένα ξενοδοχείο μπροστά από το σταθμό.

Ναι, υπάρχει ένα εστιατόριο.

Η γέφυρα είναι εκεί.

Η τράπεζα είναι δίπλα στο σχολείο.

Page 57: Word Square

taxi, bus, plane, car, train, bicycle, boat

α	λ	υ	κ	η	τ	υ	υ	α
κ	ε	τ	α	μ	σ	η	α	υ
υ	ω	τ	α	ξ	ί	σ	ε	τ
η	φ	ρ	ξ	ρ	ε	δ	ρ	ο
π	ο	δ	ή	λ	α	τ	ο	κ
ό	ρ	ν	ε	ι	τ	α	π	ί
δ	ε	ο	η	κ	ρ	ε	λ	ν
ι	ί	α	σ	λ	έ	τ	ά	η
τ	ο	η	υ	α	ν	ρ	ν	τ
λ	ε	ω	π	λ	ο	ί	ο	ο

Page 60: Which way?

1 Συγνώμη. Πώς πάω στην στάση; Ευθεία.
signómi. pos pao stin stási? efthía

2 Συγνώμη. Πώς πάω στο νοσοκομίο; Πάρτε τον πρώτο
δρόμο δεξιά. **signómi. pos pao sto nosokomío? párte ton próto**
тнrómo тнeksiá

3 Συγνώμη. Πώς πάω στην τράπεζα; Πάρτε τον πρώτο
δρόμο αριστερά. **signómi. pos pao stin trápeza? párte ton próto**
тнrómo aristerá

4 Συγνώμη. Πώς πάω στο ξενοδοχείο; Πάρτε τον δεύτερο
δρόμο δεξιά. **signómi. pos pao sto ksenoтноhío? párte ton тнeftero**
тнrómo aristerá

5 Συγνώμη. Πώς πάω στο μουσείο; Με το λεωφορείο.
signómi. pos pao sto mousío? me to leoforío

6 Συγνώμη. Πώς πάω στο αεροδρόμιο; Με το τρένο.
signómi. pos pao sto aeroтнrómio? me to tréno

Page 61: Around town

These are model answers. Yours may vary slightly.

Hotel Byron

Για το ξενοδοχείο Βύρωνας, πηγαίνετε ευθεία από εδώ. Είναι δεξιά, μετά από τον πρώτο δρόμο. **yia to ksenoτηohío víronas, piyénete efthía apo eτηó. íne τηeksiá metá apó ton próto τηrómo**

the park

Για το πάρκο, πηγαίνετε ευθεία από εδώ, πάρτε τον πρώτο δρόμο αριστερά. Είναι δίπλα δεξιά στο σχολείο. **yia to párko, piyénete efthía apo eτηó, párte ton próto τηrómo aristerá. íne τηípla sto sxolío**

the bus stop

Για την στάση, πηγαίνετε ευθεία από εδώ, πάρτε τον πρώτο δρόμο αριστερά. Είναι απέναντι από το σχολείο. **yia tin stási, piyénete efthía apo eτηó, párte ton próto τηrómo aristerá. íne apentandi apó to sxolío**

Page 62: Unscramble the conversation

f, g, d, c, a, b, e

Page 63: Game

Topic 7

Page 65: What does it mean?

Check your answers with the Key Words panel on page 64.

Page 67: Family Tree

There are many possible sentences.

If you can, check yours with a native speaker.

Page 68: Family Tree

Παύλος
Κώστας
Γιώργος

Αντρέα
Ελένη
Μαρία

Γιώργος
Κώστας
Χάρρυ

Γιάννης
Παύλος
Κώστας

Page 68: Questions and answers

1 Έχεις αδελφούς;

2 Πώς είναι το όνομα της μητέρας σου;

3 Έχεις αδελφές;

4 Πώς είναι το όνομά του αδελφού σου;

5 Πώς είναι το όνομα του πατέρα σου;

6 Πώς είναι το όνομά σου;

7 Από πού είσαι;

a Το όνομά της είναι Μαρία.

b Όχι. Δεν έχω αδελφές.

c Το όνομά του είναι Κώστας.

d Είμαι από την Χαλκίδα.

e Το όνομά μου είναι Γιώργος.

f Το όνομά του είναι Παύλος.

g Ναι. Έχω έναν αδελφό.

Page 71: How many?

οχτώ — téssera
τέσσερα — pénde
πέντε — éksi
εφτά — éna
έξι — enéa
τρία — τηéka
δύο — eftá
εννέα — októ
ένα — τηío
δέκα — tría

Page 71: Greek sums

1 τέσσερα 2 οχτώ 3 τρία 4 εννέα 5 εφτά

6 έξι 7 δέκα 8 εννέα 9 δέκα

Page 72: My family

There are many possible sentences.

If you can, check yours with a native speaker.

Answers

Topic 8

Page 75: What does it mean?

Check your answers with the Key Words panel on page 74.

Page 75: The tools of the trade

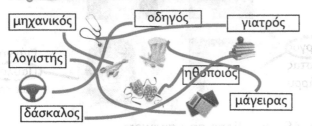

μηχανικός
οδηγός
γιατρός
λογιστής
ηθοποιός
δάσκαλος
μάγειρας

Page 77: Listen and note

1 *First name:* Maria; *Family name:* Vazaka; *Nationality:* Greek; *Spouse:* Yiorgos; *Children:* 2; *Occupation:* accountant
2 *First name:* Piero; *Family name:* Andreotti; *Nationality:* Italian; *Spouse:* Anna; *Children:* 3; *Occupation:* engineer

Page 78: What does it mean?

1d, 2c, 3e, 4a, 5b, 6f

Page 78: Which word?

Το όνομά μου είναι Χάρι και είμαι _3_. Είμαι από την Μελβούρνη στην Αυστραλία. Το όνομα της _1_ μου είναι Τζαστήν, και έχω τρία _5_: ένα _2_ και δύο _4_.

Page 80: Where do I work?

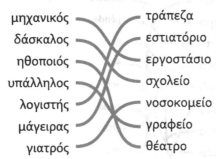

μηχανικός — τράπεζα
δάσκαλος — εστιατόριο
ηθοποιός — εργοστάσιο
υπάλληλος — σχολείο
λογιστής — νοσοκομείο
μάγειρας — γραφείο
γιατρός — θέατρο

Page 81: What are they saying?

1d, 2e, 3b, 4c, 5a, 6f

Page 82: Which word?

Το όνομά μου είναι Γιάννης Λεωνίδας. Είμαι _3_. Είμαι από την Αθήνα στην Ελλάδα, αλλά _8_ σε ένα _1_ _4_ στην Νέα Υόρκη. Η γυναίκα μου είναι _5_ και δουλεύει σε ένα μεγάλο _7_ κοντά στο εστιατόριο. Έχουμε δύο κόρες και είναι _6_ στο _2_.

Test Yourself

Page 84: I want..., please?

1 Θέλω έναν καφέ, παρακαλώ. **thélo énan kafé, parakaló**
2 Θέλω ένα κέικ, παρακαλώ. **thélo éna keik, parakaló**
3 Θέλω μια τυρόπιττα, παρακαλώ. **thélo mia tirópitta, parakaló**
4 Θέλω ένα παγωτό, παρακαλώ. **thélo éna pagotó, parakaló**
5 Θέλω ένα σάντουϊτς, παρακαλώ. **thélo éna sándouits, parakaló**

Page 85: Listen and check

1 True; 2 False; 3 True; 4 True; 5 False; 6 False

Page 85: Which word?

Το όνομά μου είναι Κατερίνα, και είμαι από την Θεσσαλονίκη, μία μεγάλη _6_ στην _8_. Είμαι δασκάλα, και δουλεύω σε ένα μικρό _3_ σχολείο στην Αγγλία. Ο άντρας μου είναι _7_, και δουλεύει σε ένα μεγάλο _5_ _1_ στο ελληνικό σχολείο. Έχουμε _4_ παιδιά, ένα _2_ και τρεις κόρες.

Page 86: Read and check

1 True; 2 True; 3 False; 4 True; 5 False; 6 True; 7 True; 8 False

Page 87: Read and check

Check your answers with the Key Words panel on page 64.

Page 87: How do you say it?

1 Ο άντρας μου είναι γιατρός. **o ándras moo íne yiatrós**
2 Έχω τέσσερα παιδιά. **ého téssera peтniá**
3 Ο γιός μας είναι μηχανικός. **o yios mas íne mihanikós**
4 Η μητέρα της Μαρίας είναι από την Αθήνα. **i mitéra tis marias íne apó tin athína**
5 Το όνομα της γυναίκας μου είναι Κλαιρ. **to ónoma tis yinékas mou íne kler**
6 Ο αδελφός μου είναι ηθοποιός. **o athelfós mou íne ithopiós**
7 Δεν έχω αδελφές. **тhen ého athelfés**
8 Έχω τρεις κόρες. **ého tris kóres**

Page 88: At the tourist office

αντίο	**adío** *goodbye*
ευχαριστώ	**efharistó** *thank you*
πίσω από	**píso apó** *behind*
δεξιά	**тнeksiá** *right*
αριστερά	**aristerá** *left*
δρόμος	**тнrómos** *street*
λεωφορείο	**leoforío** *bus*
κοντά	**kondá** *near*
μεγάλος/-η/-ο	**megálos/-i/-o** *big*
μουσείο	**moosío** *museum*
πού	**poo** *where*
καλημέρα	**kaliméra** *good morning*

Name cards:

Γιώργο(ς)	Άννα	Κώστα(ς)	Μαρία
Ελίζαμπεθ	Ανν	Μαίρη	Κάθριν
Χάρρυ	Μάικλ	Ντέϊβιντ	Τζων

Sentence-build cards:

;	το όνομά μου	κύριε	είναι
.	το όνομά σου	ευχαριστώ	καλημέρα
αντίο	το όνομά σας	παρακαλώ	καλησπέρα
πώς	κύρια	γειά σας	γειά σου

Maria	Kosta(s)	Anna	Yiorgo(s)
Catherine	Mary	Ann	Elizabeth
John	David	Michael	Harry

is	Mr.	my name	?
good morning	thank you	your name *(informal)*	.
good evening	please	your name *(polite)*	goodbye
hello *(informal)*	hello *(polite)*	Mrs.	what

GAME CARD ❸ (see page 33)

Picture cards:

Cut-out pictures (cut round small pictures)

Sentence-build cards:

πάνω από τον	δίπλα στον	κάτω από τον	στον
πάνω από το	δίπλα στο	κάτω από το	στο
πάνω από την	δίπλα στην	κάτω από την	στην
καναπές	κρεβάτι	τραπέζι	καρέκλα
ένα σάντουϊτς	ένα κάδρο	ένα τηλέφωνο	ένα κομπιούτερ
Υπάρχει	μία γάτα	ένα ποντίκι	μία τηλεόραση

in/on the *(masculine)*	under the *(masculine)*	next to the *(masculine)*	above the *(masculine)*
in/on the *(neuter)*	under the *(neuter)*	next to the *(neuter)*	above the *(neuter)*
in/on the *(feminine)*	under the *(feminine)*	next to the *(feminine)*	above the *(feminine)*
chair	table	bed	sofa
a computer	a telephone	a picture	a sandwich
a television	a mouse	a cat	There's

Picture cards:

Adjective cards:

μεγάλος	μικρός	καινούριος	παλιός
ακριβός	φτηνός	αργός	γρήγορος
όμορφος	άσκημος	παράξενος	μακρύς

Picture cards:

You are here

τέσσερα	ένα	εφτά	εννέα
δέκα	οχτώ	τρία	δύο
οχτώ	έξι	εφτά	ένα
έξι	εννέα	τέσσερα	έξι

δύο	ένα	τρία	δύο
τρία	πέντε	έξι	εφτά
οχτώ	πέντε	δέκα	εννέα
τρία	τέσσερα	εφτά	τρία

1
2
3
4
5
6
7
8
9
10

Picture cards:

Profession cards:

δάσκαλος	λογιστής	γιατρός	οδηγός
ηθοποιός	μάγειρας	υπάλληλος	μάγειρας
φοιτητής			